The Economics of Agriculture

David Metcalf

Penguin Books

Penguin Books Ltd, Harmondsworth,
Middlesex, England
Penguin Books Inc., 7110 Ambassador Road,
Baltimore, Md 21207, U.S.A.
Penguin Books Australia Ltd, Ringwood,
Victoria, Australia

First published 1969
Copyright © David Metcalf, 1969

Made and printed in Great Britain by
Cox & Wyman Ltd, London, Reading and Fakenham
Set in Monotype Times

Penguin Modern Economics Texts

This volume is one in a series of unit texts designed to reduce the price of knowledge for students of economics in universities and colleges of higher education. The units may be used singly or in combination with other units to form attractive and unusual teaching programmes. The volumes will cover the major teaching areas but they will differ from conventional books in their attempt to chart and explore new directions in economic thinking. The traditional divisions of theory and applied, of positive and normative and of micro and macro will tend to be blurred as authors impose new and arresting ideas on the traditional corpus of economics. Some units will fall into conventional patterns of thought but many will transgress established beliefs.

Penguin Modern Economics Texts are published in units in order to achieve certain objectives. First, a large range of short texts at inexpensive prices gives the teacher flexibility in planning his course and recommending texts for it. Secondly, the pace at which important new work is published requires the project to be adaptable. Our plan allows a unit to be revised or a fresh unit to be added with maximum speed and minimal cost to the reader.

The international range of authorship will, it is hoped, bring out the richness and diversity in economic analysis and thinking.

B.J.MCC.

To my parents

Contents

Editorial Foreword

In the world as a whole most people are farmers or farm workers, and most people depend upon agriculture for their well-being. There is therefore no need to search far for explanation of the importance always attached to the study of the economics of agriculture. This study has been undertaken by two types of economist: those with a training as agriculturalists who devote their main attention to finding means for improving farm efficiency, and, secondly, applied economists who deploy economic analysis in order to deal with problems of growing, rearing, processing and marketing farm products.

The first group of agriculturalist-economists have made important contributions to economic knowledge as well as to farming practice. They are responsible for more being known about processes of production, structures of costs and consequent conditions of supply in agriculture than in any other industry. Similarly, there are more studies of the responsiveness of demand to price and income changes for agricultural than for other products. Agricultural economics thus provides a means for students to learn production and demand theory in real-life situations.

Applied economists whose boots are not so muddy as those of the first group have devoted attention to agriculture as a scene of rapid change and increasing productivity. All advanced countries have witnessed the continuous migration of workers out of agriculture into other occupations. At the same time output per head has risen fast for those remaining in the industry. Students of economic growth have a special interest in agriculture.

There are in addition more traditional concerns with the effects of market structure on conduct and performance. Farming has provided favourite examples of perfect competition; but with government regulation it has also provided many examples of cartels, and beyond the growing stage, in processing and marketing, other structures are to be found.

Finally, there are policies of agricultural support which almost all governments implement. They provide classic examples of attempts to stabilize prices and incomes and of the incompatibility of price stability with income stability.

David Metcalf – lecturer in economics, and consultant to agriculture's Little Neddy and the Monopolies Commission – is well suited to act as a guide to these main areas of agricultural economics. He has experience of teaching these subjects at the London School of Economics to audiences removed a remarkable distance from the land. This may be why he is able to make complicated subjects clear to the novice without descending to trivialization. A very valuable feature of this book is the demonstration it provides of the power of economic analysis to clarify applied problems. It should help economic students in general as well as those specializing in applied economics, industrial economics and agricultural economics. Lay readers will find that they are not left far behind in the technical parts and that there is a good deal to interest them in the policy sections.

H.T.

Preface

This book is designed as an introduction to agricultural economics for students who have previously taken an introductory course in economics.

It has not been possible to cover all aspects of the subject. I am conscious of omitting some traditional portions of agricultural economics such as land tenure and credit problems. I have included those parts of the subject, both descriptive and analytical, which I would teach in an introductory course. About half the book is devoted to an examination of factor and product markets which reflects the fact that I consider that these subjects have been somewhat neglected in the past.

I am indebted to David Colman, Keith Cowling, Christine Greenhalgh, Tim Josling and, especially, Harry Townsend for helpful comments on an earlier draft; and to my wife, Helen, for help with proof reading and indexing. I am, of course, responsible for all remaining short-comings and mistakes.

1 Theory of the Farm Firm

In the first sections of this chapter, the production decisions facing the individual farmer are analysed theoretically. There are three types of decision: first, *resource–product* (single input) problems, for example, determining the most profitable amount of a resource to use in the production of a commodity; second, *resource–resource* (multiple input) decisions such as determining the most profitable combination of resources to produce a specific amount of a given output; third, *product–product* decisions, for example, what is the most profitable mix of products to produce from the available supply of inputs.

The remaining sections of the chapter look at the economics of farm size and the problem of imperfect knowledge which also bears on the farmer's production decisions.

Resource–Product Relationships

The relationship between resources (inputs) and products (outputs) can be characterized as a *production function*, for example,

$$Y = f(X_1, X_2, \ldots, X_n) \qquad 1$$

where Y is the quantity produced of some output over some time period and X_1 to X_n are the quantities of the factors employed in producing this output; this is a technological concept referring to physical quantities of inputs and outputs – once the input level and mix has been chosen the maximum possible output is given by the function. We must distinguish here between fixed and variable inputs. For example, if the decision facing the farmer is how much fertilizer to be used in grain production, he may consider the other inputs as fixed. The production function may then be written

$$Y = f(X_1 \mid X_2, \ldots, X_n) \qquad 2$$

where Y is output of grain, X_1 is the variable fertilizer input and X_2 to X_n are the fixed inputs. This production function **2** does not state by how much the output of Y changes as the quantity of the variable input is changed; to express the quantitative relationship between inputs and outputs the production function must be expressed algebraically, for example $Y = a + bX_1$, which states that output Y is a linear function of input X_1.

The production function is a technological relationship between input and output; as long as technology remains constant the production function remains unchanged and indicates the greatest output from a given input mix. Economic considerations involving input prices (firms' costs) and product prices (firms' revenue) are *not* part of a production function. The production function therefore constitutes one part of the decision problem facing the firm, the other part depending upon input and output prices.

The production decision regarding the amount of the variable input to be used hinges on the *law of diminishing returns*, which states: *if the input of one resource is increased by equal increments per unit of time while the inputs of other resources are held constant, total product will increase, but beyond some point the resulting output increases will become smaller and smaller.*

An empirical example of this law is given in Table 1. The

Table 1
Law of Diminishing Returns

Units of nitrogen fertilizer used	Total corn yield per acre	Additional corn for each additional unit of fertilizer
(1)	(2)	(3)
(20 lb units)	(bushels)	(bushels)
0	26·0	—
1	38·0	12·0
2	42·0	4·0
3	43·3	1·3
4	44·0	0·7

Source: Vincent (1962), p. 42.

variable input is nitrogen fertilizer (column 1), which is added to fixed amounts of land and other inputs. Corn yield per acre (column 2), gets larger as successive units of nitrogen fertilizer are applied, but the increase in yield (column 3) becomes smaller for each incremental increase in fertilizer application.

The law of diminishing returns is explained more fully in Table 2. The first column indicates the units of the variable resource X used, the second the total output Y, the third, the average output per unit of variable factor Y/X, and the fourth the change in Y as a consequence of adding a further unit of X, with all other factor inputs fully utilized and fixed. It can be seen that (a) increments of X beyond the fourth add successively less to total product, (b) the average product continues to increase as long as the marginal product lies above it, that is, up to five units of X, (c) the additional unit of input beyond the seventh causes the total product to decline, the marginal product therefore being negative.

Table 2
Units of Variable Input and Corresponding Total, Average and Marginal Products

Input (X)	Total product (Y)	Average product (Y/X)	Marginal product ($\triangle Y/\triangle X$)
0	0	—	
1	4	4	4
2	10	5	6
3	18	6	8
4	28	7	10
5	36	$7\frac{1}{5}$	8
6	41	$6\frac{5}{6}$	5
7	42	6	1
8	40	5	—2

The total, average and marginal products of Table 2 are

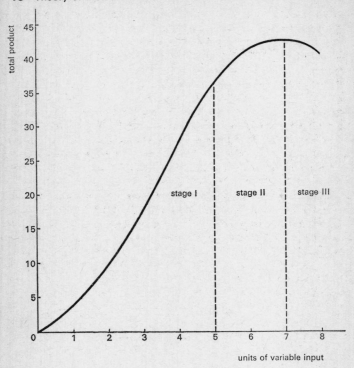

Figure 1 Total, average and marginal

shown graphically in Figure 1, where the input–output relationship is divided into three stages.[1] This division of the production function into three stages enables us, for the profit maximizing farmer, to eliminate, from knowledge of this physical data alone, two of the stages as irrational areas of production, assuming the product price P_y and variable

1. Although the production function was derived from discrete input–output observations, it is assumed that the function is continuous, and the points are therefore joined on the graph.

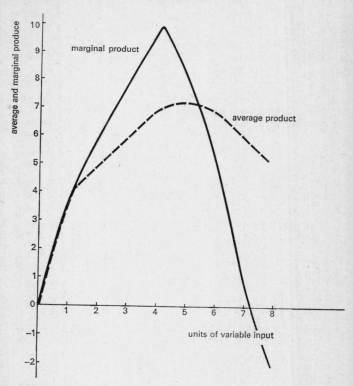

product and the stages of production

input price P_x are constant, as they typically will be for any given farmer.

Stage I of the production function continues up to that level of input at which the average product is at a maximum, an input of five units of X; the marginal product up to this point is thus always greater than the average product. Therefore, if it is profitable to produce any output then the farmer can make greater profit from using more X as long as the average product increases. For the profit maximizing farmer to produce in stage I is thus irrational. An example of farmers producing in this stage is dairy farmers in some areas of the U.K., where the variable input of nitrogenous fertilizer is not applied in sufficient quantity, probably because of lack of experience in applying it, lack of information or uncertainty as to the results.

Stage III is similarly irrational. The farmer is incurring greater costs, as he is utilizing more X, but is simultaneously receiving less revenue YP_y because each additional unit of X results in a decline in total output, the marginal product of X being negative.[1] This occurs, for example, when crops are planted too close together. Therefore from *physical* production function data we can infer that for a profit maximizing farmer the best level of resource use occurs in stage II, between five and seven units of X in our example. The actual position in this stage of the production function (quantity of the variable input used) chosen by the profit maximizing producer depends upon the *economic* factors of product and input prices; profits will be maximized where the value of the marginal product produced by the incremental input equals the price of the input, including where relevant the cost of applying it.

Resource–Resource Relationships

In this section we are concerned with a production function of the type

$$Y_1 = f(X_1, X_2 \mid X_3 \ldots, X_n)$$

where two, or more, factors of production are variable. We are interested here both in what happens to output as the quantities of both variable inputs are increased or decreased and in the substitution of one variable factor for another. At the technical unit level, for example one animal, the variable inputs might be two feed types, forage and grain, or inputs of seed and fertilizer might be variable with respect to one acre of land. At the farm level labour and capital are substitutable over a certain number of acres or animals. The resource–resource relationships

1. If the price of the marginal stage III units of the variable input is zero, as it might be in the case of water inputs, then the farmer will not be incurring extra costs.

will be described geometrically in terms of two variable inputs.

Just as there are irrational and rational production techniques in the resource–product relationships so there are in resource–resource relations. Consider Figure 2.

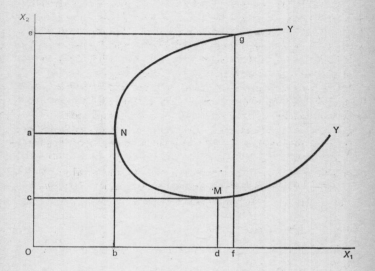

Figure 2 The rational and irrational input combinations

It can be seen that output Y can be produced by a large number of combinations of the variable inputs X_1 and X_2. The line describing such combinations (or bundles) of variable factors producing a given output is termed an isoquant (*iso* = equal, *quant* = quantity) or isoproduct curve. A rational, profit maximizing farmer would never use the combination of variable inputs Of of X_1 and Oe of X_2 for there are other input bundles requiring less of *both* factors which will produce the same output. Rather, the choice of input bundles facing a rational farmer occurs along the NM segment of the isoquant. If the farmer uses more than Oa of X_2 he will also require more than Ob of X_1, if he uses more than Od of X_1 he will also need to use more than Oc of X_2 to produce output Y. The factors are only technical substitutes for one another over the range NM; outside the NM portion of the isoquant they become technically complementary.[1]

To determine the level of input-use and the least-cost combination of inputs data on the price of inputs are needed. This will show the different bundles of X_1 and X_2 that the farmer can purchase. Assume a dairy farmer with two variable inputs, feed (X_1) and labour (X_2). The problem facing the farmer is to use inputs X_1 and X_2 in such proportions that for any given output the cost outlay on X_1 and X_2 will be as small as possible. This can be put the other way round: the farmer should use that bundle of X_1 and X_2 which will produce the greatest output for a given cost outlay. Assume the price of X_1 is £2 and the price of X_2 is £1. The cost outlay to be made by the farmer on these two variable inputs is £33 per day. The daily marginal physical product schedules in stage II for X_1 and X_2 are indicated in Table 3.

Table 3

Optimum Input Bundle

Resource X_1 (Physical units)	MPP_{x1} (Units of Y)	Resource X_2 (Physical units)	MPP_{x2} (Units of Y)
10	20	4	12
11	18	5	10
12	16	6	8
13	12	7	6
14	6	8	2
15	0	9	0

1. The rational area of production is then defined along that portion of the isoquant where the lines drawn parallel to the X_1 and X_2 axes are tangential to the isoquant.

The farmer maximizes total output by distributing his cost outlay (£33) among X_1 and X_2 such that the MPP of a pound's worth of one resource equals the MPP of a pound's worth of the other. Let P_{x1} equal the price of one unit of X_1 and P_{x2} equal the price of one unit of X_2. Then to maximize output from a given cost outlay it is necessary that

$$\frac{\text{MPP}_{x1}}{P_{x1}} = \frac{\text{MPP}_{x2}}{P_{x2}} .$$

The price of X_1 is £2 and the price of X_2 is £1. Therefore the bundle of inputs used should be such that the MPP of X_1 is twice that of X_2 for a cost outlay of £33. Therefore the farmer should use thirteen units of X_1 and seven units of X_2. At these input levels the MPP per pound's worth of each input is six units of output.

The student should verify that output is maximized for the given cost outlay by this input combination by calculating what happens to output if a pound is shifted from X_1 to X_2 or vice versa.

The over-all picture of the least-cost combination with two variable inputs is shown in Figure 3 which presents a map of isoquants. The rational area of resource-mix occurs for any given output on the portions of the isoquants between the lines OA and OB.[1] The parallel lines ab, cd, ef, gh are *factor cost* or *isocost* curves. If the amount necessary to hire Ob of X_1 were used to hire resource X_2, then Oa could be purchased. The slope of ab indicates the price of X_1 in terms of X_2, and all points on ab represent the same total cost. The greatest total output that can be produced from an outlay represented by the isocost line ab is determined by the point of tangency (S) between ab and an isoquant, in this case an output of 1Y. Thus

1. OA and OB are termed *isoclines*, that is, they are lines joining the points of equal slope on successive isoquants. These particular isoclines, which define the rational range of input mixes are termed *ridge lines*. Rational producers will never operate to the left of OA or to the right of OB.

the lowest total cost at which 1Y can be produced is by using Op units of X_1 and Or units of X_2[1].

If the firm decides to quadruple output to 4Y the lowest cost combination of factors would be determined by the point of tangency between an isocost curve and the isoquant 4Y, that

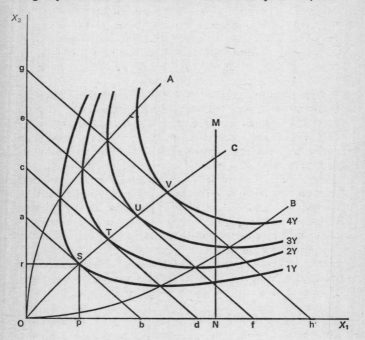

Figure 3 Optimum input combinations

1. Point S is then the least-cost input combination to produce 1Y. At any given point on the isoquant 1Y the marginal rate of substitution of X_1 for X_2 is equal to MPP_{x_1}/MPP_{x_2} and is also equal to the slope of the isoquant at that point. At point S the slope of isoquant 1Y equals the slope of the isocost line ab tangential to it at that point, which equals P_{x_1}/P_{x_2}. Therefore at point S $MPP_{x_1}/MPP_{x_2} = P_{x_1}/P_{x_2}$, and by manipulation $MPP_{x_1}/P_{x_1} = MPP_{x_2}/P_{x_2}$. The analogy between this section and the conventional treatment of consumer demand using indifference curves and a budget constraint should now be obvious.

is, combination V in the diagram. If input prices remain unchanged, that is, the slope of the isocost lines are unchanged, the lowest cost combinations of X_1 and X_2 as output is increased are traced by the isocline OC (through the tangency points S, T, U, V). This curve is known as the *expansion path*, indicating the lowest cost combinations of variable factors of production for successive output levels. If relative factor prices change, say labour X_1 becomes dearer relative to tractors X_2, then the slope of the isocost curve will change, in this instance becoming steeper and the least-cost input-bundles to produce a given output will change.

Figure 3 also indicates whether increasing, constant or decreasing returns to scale are operating. Pure scale considerations involve situations where the inputs are all increased at the same rate. Figure 3 indicates that for this 2-input case there are constant returns to scale, in that the distance between the isoquants out along the expansion path OC are constant: if all factor inputs are doubled (trebled, etc.) output is doubled (trebled, etc.). Increasing returns to scale would be described by successively *smaller* distances between the isoquants along the expansion path, and decreasing returns by successively *greater* increases. The diagram also indicates that for any one factor the law of diminishing returns operates. Consider the line NM. Input of X_1 is fixed at ON and it is seen from the line NM that increases in output by constant amounts require more than proportional increases in the variable input X_2.

Product–Product Relationships

The third production decision is that involving product–product relationships, that is, decisions as to which crops and/or livestock should be produced from the available stock of inputs. The mechanics of this production decision are described in Figure 4. For ease of exposition we deal with two outputs, Y_1 and Y_2; the analysis of this decision will be brief as the reasoning is similar to that presented in the previous section.

The production-possibility curve (or transformation or iso-resource curve) cd describes the bundles of commodities which can be produced with a set of given inputs. Assuming, as is normally the case, that Y_1 and Y_2 are both being produced in areas of the production function having decreasing marginal returns, the marginal rate of substitution between the commodities Y_1 and Y_2 will be increasing, that is, successive increments in the production of Y_1 (or Y_2) require increasing sacrifices in the production of Y_2, (or Y_1). If smaller quantities of inputs are available the curve will shift towards the origin; alternatively it will be shifted outwards as more resources become available.

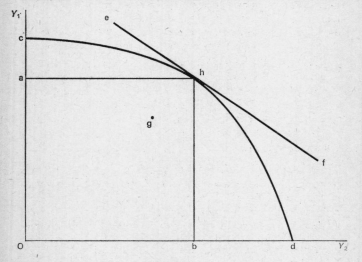

Figure 4   Optimum product combinations

The profit maximizing firm will not produce at point g as, with resource input constant, more of Y_1 could be produced without sacrifice of Y_2, and vice versa, or up to a point more of both commodities could be produced. Thus no knowledge of the prices of Y_1 and Y_2 is necessary to state that to produce at point g is both technically and economically inefficient. However, to specify the best (profit maximizing) bundle of outputs from all the possible choices of combinations presented by cd, that is, those using technically efficient production techniques, knowledge of the prices of Y_1 and Y_2 is needed.

Diagrammatically, to determine the best (maximum profit) bundle of commodities to produce, it is necessary to superimpose the *isorevenue* curve ef on to the production-possibility curve. The isorevenue curve defines the bundles of Y_1 and Y_2 which bring in an equal revenue, the slope of the curve denoting the ratio of prices between the two products. The aim of a profit maximizing farmer is to achieve the highest possible revenue line, which is attained at the point of tangency between the two curves. Substitution of Y_2 for Y_1 is always profitable as long as the slope of the production possibility curve is less than the slope of the isorevenue curve, namely to the north-west of the point of tangency h. Conversely, south-east of h Y_1 should be substituted for Y_2. The optimum combination of output, for this given technical production-possibility curve and producer-price ratio, is to produce Oa of Y_1 and Ob of Y_2, where the marginal product of a unit of resource allocated to the production of Y_1 or Y_2 is equal.[1]

Economics of Farm Size

Let us at this point, having introduced resource–product and resource–resource relationships, now consider the economics of the size of farm business. It is necessary to distinguish between scale and proportionality relationships. *Pure scale* relationships occur when *all* inputs are increased or decreased at the same rate, and therefore involve long-run production functions in which no factors are fixed. Patently, such a situation will only occur rarely in agriculture because of the difficulties in varying the inputs of management and land. Whilst the farmer may be able to increase all other inputs by, say, one fifth, he can only increase his own managerial effort if his skill, ability and energy were not fully employed. When some resources are fixed and others variable, involving a short-run

1. This can be demonstrated algebraically. In the section on the law of diminishing marginal returns it was shown that for profit maximization the variable resource X should be employed in the production of Y_1 up to the point where its MVP is equal to its price, $MVP_x(Y_1) = P_x$. Similarly for Y_2 it is necessary that $MVP_x(Y_2) = P_x$.
   Therefore $MVP_x(Y_1) = MVP_x(Y_2)$.

production function, or if employment of all factors is increased or decreased, but at different rates, then the changes in the input–output relationships are not ones of pure scale, but rather involve *variable proportions*.

These two facets of the economics of farm size will be analysed from the viewpoint of increasing farm size, which is a major policy problem in most countries. First, returns to scale; *increasing* returns (percentage increase in output greater than the percentage increase in inputs) may come about through specialization. Assume a fifty-acre farm on which the operator divides his own management/labour input between dairy, pig and poultry enterprises. Now assume a tripling of farm size to 150 acres, *each* of the three enterprises being three times as large, and of sufficient size to have a specialist operator, in which case output may well be greater than three times the original output. If output is increased by exact replication then we might expect *constant* returns to scale; for example, one operator and a 100-pig farm building and associated feed inputs exactly replicated would be likely to produce the original output times the number of replications. Decreasing returns might come about because the increment of land in the expanded input mix is spatially more distant, requiring more time to transport the inputs and products; alternatively, for livestock decreasing returns could result from greater incidence of disease as herd size expands.[1]

Second, and far more common, farm size can be increased by expanding the employment of some factors, with intake of others fixed or falling, or by increasing the employment of all factors, but at differing rates. Typically, inputs of capital and hired labour occur in indivisible units, in contrast to a perfectly divisible factor such as fertilizer. Thus one operator may be fully employed on a 100-acre dairy farm. If the farm acreage is

1. Some exception may be taken to the examples of increasing and decreasing returns to scale. In the former it could be argued that the management input has increased more than proportionately. In the latter it could be argued that the land input was not increased in the same proportion because it is more distant. This amounts to saying that if all inputs are properly specified there can probably only ever be constant returns to scale.

now increased to 120, with the same stocking rate, it will not be possible, except through the use of part-time or casual labour to employ 1½ man, and if two men are now employed costs will increase proportionately more than output.[1] Conversely costs will be reduced relative to output if an indivisible machinery input is equally well able to cope with say, an increase in arable area from 200 to 300 acres. If, however, existing machinery is unable to cope with the increased size then further indivisible capital inputs, unemployed for much of the time, will be needed. Some smaller farmers overcome this indivisibility problem by co-operative ownership and operation of large capital items such as combine-harvesters and grain driers which save them separately incurring the costs of these indivisible inputs or using more expensive contracting services.

The timing of factor substitutions, typically capital for labour, depends on factor prices, as we saw in the section on resource–resource decisions. Capital-intensive production techniques typically have high fixed costs per acre, such as depreciation, taxation and storage; but variable costs, e.g. petrol and operators' time, are generally lower than when more labour-intensive techniques are used. Substitution of capital for labour becomes profitable when the increase in fixed costs is less than the additional variable costs of using the labour-intensive technique.

This brief review of the economics of farm size prompts the question, 'Why do farms of different sizes persist?' Agriculture provides the best example of an industry approximating to the norm of perfect competition. Under such a market structure the firm must minimize its long-run costs and use the least-cost production technique, or the return on the resources will be less than they could earn elsewhere. It seems strange then that the diversity of farm size continues; from both a technological viewpoint, i.e. looking at the physical input combinations, and an economic one, i.e. allowing for changes in relative factor prices, it appears that small farms are becoming less viable.

1. The increase in unit costs caused by the employment of the extra man will of course be smaller the larger the number of men already fully employed.

There is therefore a need to explain the persistence of small farms which are alleged to be uneconomic.

Among the explanations are: first, farmers may not be 'rational' in that they may have an alternative objective to profit maximization, maximizing satisfaction rather than profit, for example. Second, whilst returns to some resources, notably to the small farmer's own labour, appear low they may in fact be *greater* than the operator could earn elsewhere; this is almost certainly so for some older farmers who are unwilling or unable to be retrained and are unable to get employment in construction or other industries to which migrants move. Third, in times or areas of high unemployment the farm will provide greater employment opportunities for the farm family than are available in other occupations. In view of this they may accept low wages which discourages the substitution of capital for labour. Fourth, the farmer may face a budget constraint; after paying rent or interest he may have insufficient funds to increase the size of the farm business. He may still be prepared to remain in the industry, despite higher costs than other farmers, in the hope of accumulating sufficient capital to adopt the optimum production techniques. However, it is well known that big operators are able to get credit more easily than small operators, and they are therefore able to outbid the smaller operators in the land market, making it more difficult for small farmers to attain optimum size. Fifth, farmers may decide against large-scale production because it involves the possibility of large losses with falling product prices. This cause of the persistence of small farms is less important for countries operating schemes which guarantee minimum agricultural prices. The problem of taking account of uncertainty in making production decisions is the subject of the next section. Finally, some farmers may simply be unaware of alternative employment opportunities, or have a fear of urban life.

All these are plausible explanations of a short-run disequilibrium situation: resources remain in the industry when they could earn more elsewhere. However, there must be at least a profit constraint, for example, profits must be greater than zero or equal to some minimum specified amount. The resources cannot remain in the industry indefinitely without at least some return.

The Problem of Imperfect Knowledge

The problem of imperfect knowledge has an important bearing on decisions taken by farmers. For example, when purchasing durable inputs the farmer should continue his purchases up to the point where the present value of the discounted stream of future earnings equals the price of the input. However, the farmer's expectation of the present value of the stream of future returns depends critically on the level of product prices which he expects to prevail in the future.

There are four elements involved in the farmer's decision-making process. First, his *objective*, Z: the traditional theory of the firm assumes the objective is to maximize profits but an individual farmer may prefer an alternative objective, for example to have a lower average level of profit which is subject to less variance than a more variable higher average level, or he may have some other objective or target such as maximizing his satisfaction. Next, there are *decision variables*, X, that is, choices of action subject to control by the farmer, the options open to move him closer towards his objective, for example the production possibilities, the combinations of inputs and outputs. Third, there are *events* or uncontrolled variables, Y, for example the weather is outside the control of the farmer; also farmers tend to operate in a market structure which approximates to perfect competition and therefore the unit product price he receives for a product of a given quality is totally unaffected by any actions he or any other individual farmer might take[1]. Similarly, he will be influenced by certain psychological factors largely outside his control such as his background and number of dependents to support. Lastly, we need a *mechanism* linking the above elements together,

1. The more concentrated the market the more the actions of an individual producer will affect that market, in which case the important exogenous element becomes not the market structure but the behaviour of competitors.

i.e. $Z = f(X, Y)$. If there were no exogenous factors affecting output and price then the only determinant of whether the farmer succeeds in maximizing his objective function, Z, would be the X variables, but as fluctuations in output and price do occur because certain factors are uncontrollable we wish to know the consequences which flow from the combination of the producer's actions and exogenous events. Let us look at the problem of imperfect knowledge, the Y variables, in more detail.

The farmer makes his production decisions with imperfect knowledge of the outcome of these decisions, which can lead to his income being lower or more variable than it would be with improved knowledge of the future. Where do risk and uncertainty occur in agriculture? There are two major types of imperfect knowledge, both of which result from environmental circumstances outside the control of the farmer. First, *yield* is uncertain. Yield variation is likely to be greater in some regions than in others, for example tropical areas as against temperate areas. The yield of certain crops, for example cotton, is also more variable than that of other crops such as wheat. But the individual farmer is unable to forecast accurately the output which will be obtained from the particular mix of inputs he employs; this is because agriculture is a biological industry and the outputs of crops, animals and animal products are more dependent on weather, insects and disease than the products of other industries.

Second, uncertainty exists as to the *prices of the final product*. The supply of agricultural products fluctuates because of factors such as weather and disease and this, when coupled with a demand for agricultural products which is inelastic with respect to both price and income, causes large fluctuations in agricultural product prices. This sort of uncertainty is mitigated, more or less, by buffer stock schemes which cause the elasticity of demand to move towards unity, so stabilizing income, or by guaranteed prices schemes.

It will be noted that the two types of uncertainty are, at the market or over-all level, offsetting, a lower yield over all farmers leading to a higher product price and vice versa; also a change in yield and/or price might induce acreage adjustments between crops.

The problem of product price and yield uncertainty is accentuated for the farmer because certain farm outputs, notably feed grains, are inputs for other farm enterprises. Livestock farmers may therefore be reluctant to expand their herds because of uncertainty as to the availability and price of feedingstuffs.

A third, but minor, form of uncertainty may exist as to the likely prices and quality of inputs. This is primarily of importance for capital inputs, which are costly and may be subject to rapid qualitative improvements, which might cause farmers to postpone purchases of such inputs.

What do past studies suggest about farmers' expectations and reactions to uncertainty?[1] There is some evidence that farmers are optimistic that 'favourable' *weather* will prevail in the current year if previously there had been a run of 'poor' weather. As the number of years having poor weather increases the degree of surprise attributable to another poor year increases. On *prices* studies suggest that farmers are conservative, adopting that course of action which maximizes returns or minimizes losses in the least favourable year. The adoption of this strategy is justified if the farmer is pessimistic, or if he is unable to follow a strategy which might yield higher returns but might also yield lower returns. This latter would be the case if the farmer must aim for some assured level of income to look after his family or pay mortgage interest. On *yields*, studies suggest farmers are neither optimistic nor pessimistic as to future yields, but rather anticipate in any one year a similar yield to the average of those prevailing over the last few years.

What use is the study of decision making under uncertainty in agriculture? It is sometimes claimed that an analysis of farmers' decisions in the face of uncertainty aids in the *prescription* of certain strategies to farmers. However, this is not always the case. Farm extension workers might suggest that a farmer could raise his income by changing his management technique and production decisions; but this presupposes that

1. For a survey of some major studies see Cowling and Perkins (1963).

the farmer is able to face similar risks and uncertainties as those farmers already operating the particular production decisions advised. The extension worker needs to take account of the farmer's attitude to risk which presupposes knowledge of the farmer's psychological make-up.

The main use of the analysis of decision making in agriculture is for *prediction*. For example, if studies suggest farmers wish to minimize the risk of yield variation, we can predict that they will adopt a particular kind of seed or animal. This provides useful knowledge for seed companies or animal breeding institutes. Similarly, if farmers have pessimistic expectations about product prices, this will encourage them to diversify their enterprises, which is useful knowledge, say, for a government which is encouraging greater specialization.

Finally, let us briefly summarize the different methods by which farmers can overcome the uncertainty as to the future, each method involving the cost that profit *might* in fact have been higher had the farmer not troubled to mitigate uncertainty. First, it is possible for the farmer to *insure* against certain risks such as loss due to poor weather, insect infestation and disease. The farmer chooses to incur a small known cost, the insurance premium, in order to transfer the risk of a much larger loss to someone else. Second, farmers can provide their own insurance through *diversification*, that is, having more than one enterprise on the farm and/or ensuring crops are produced and sold over differing time spans. Such diversification is likely to reduce the variation in the farmers' aggregate income as generally yields and prices of all products do not vary in the same direction simultaneously. Third, farmers can ensure that their production techniques are *flexible*. If they anticipate that the price of a commodity is likely to rise shortly it will pay them to be able to switch resources into that enterprise (providing of course that not *all* or even a large proportion of farmers have sufficiently flexible production techniques to do likewise). To achieve this flexibility it is important that the farmers' capital investment on farm buildings is not of too specialized a nature, but can be adapted for use in more than one enterprise, for example poultry houses which can be used both by broilers and layers.

Similarly, dual-purpose cows provide the farmer with more flexibility than specialized milk or beef animals. To ensure flexibility it may also be necessary for the farmer to hold more liquid assets than he otherwise would. Lastly, uncertainty as to product prices can be overcome by making *contractual arrangements* with food processors which guarantee the farmer a certain price for a given grade of product at a given time. These marketing arrangements are analysed more fully in chapter 5.

2 Resource Structure and the Demand for Inputs

Introduction

The resource structure, or input mix, of the agricultural sector has changed substantially in most advanced countries through time, and will continue to do so in the future. In this chapter we first describe the changing pattern of agricultural input-use in the U.S.A. and U.K. We then set up a model of one factor market, the agricultural labour market, and indicate how the variables used in the model aid understanding of movement of workers away from farming. Next, drawing evidence from econometric studies, we indicate some of the factors which have been responsible for the growth in the demand for capital inputs, using as an example farm buildings, and for current inputs, using fertilizer as an example. Agricultural factor markets were neglected in comparison with other branches of agricultural economics until comparatively recently and inferences drawn from the research studies on factor markets should perhaps be viewed with caution.

Studies indicating the variables which influence the demand for factors have a number of uses. First, they attempt to account for changes in the quantity of a particular input used. Second, they provide a source of agricultural supply estimates which is important in view of the very real difficulties of estimating aggregate supply relationships directly. There is often a large discrepancy between *planned* and *realized* output because of the year-to-year weather variations. The structural relationships underlying the demand for a particular input, when coupled with similar information for other inputs aid in estimation of the planned (as opposed to realized) aggregate agricultural supply function. For example, it may be found that a *w* per cent rise in agricultural product prices will cause the agricultural sector to employ *x* per cent more labour, *y* per cent more capital and *z* per cent more fertilizer. Using estimates of the effect of these inputs on output in average weather conditions, it is possible to gain an indirect measure of the (planned) elasticity of supply of agricultural product with respect to changes in product prices.

Third, the studies aid in assessing the impact of government policy on agriculture. The agricultural industries of most advanced countries have been subject to continuous public intervention in the post-war period; this intervention affects the demand for inputs via price support for agricultural products, tariffs and subsidies on the inputs. Part of this chapter is devoted to indicating the policy implications derived from the study of agricultural factor markets. We examine the direct effect of agricultural policy, and the indirect effects on agriculture of general economic policy.

Fourth, analysis of the structural relationships underlying the demand for a particular input in a given country is relevant in assessing the future demand and changing trends of demand for the input. Fifth, identification of the factors influencing the demand for an input in an advanced country is useful knowledge for developing nations. Sixth, many input industries have oligopolistic market structures. Studies on inputs can generate information on these oligopolistic supply situations by examining changes in the quality of inputs or in the quantity used following advertising campaigns.

The Changing Pattern of Resource Structure

Tables 4 and 5 indicate the changing patterns of resource use in the agricultural sectors of the U.S.A. and U.K. Table 4 shows the quantities of inputs utilized by the American agricultural industry. The three main features of this table are first, the decline, by more than half, in the labour input over the fifty years 1910–60. Next, the enormous increase in the use of capital inputs in the years since 1920. Third, the increase, although somewhat less spectacular than that of capital items, in the use of purchased inputs such as fertilizer, feed and seed.

Table 4
Index of Major Categories of Inputs for Selected Years, 1910–60, U.S.A. (1947–9 = 100)

Resource category	1910	1920	1930	1940	1950	1960
Farm labour	135	143	137	122	90	62
Machinery and power	28	44	55	58	118	142
Farm buildings	99	116	111	98	106	128
Fertilizer and lime	20	28	36	48	118	192
Tractors	—	9	32	55	119	133
Combines	—	1	12	37	137	205
Cornpickers	—	—	17	36	151	251
Feed, seed and livestock purchased	22	32	37	63	101	149
Miscellaneous capital operating items	71	85	96	93	108	138
Cropland	87	95	103	100	100	92

Source: Heady and Tweeten (1963), p. 15.

A similar trend can be seen from Table 5 which presents details of the changing proportion of farm *expenditures* on different inputs in the U.K. It can be seen that the proportion of expenditure on labour declined by over half in the post-war period, and that on machinery has risen significantly from its pre-war figure.

The above tables bring out not just the substitution of capital inputs for labour but also indicate the substitution of purchased inputs for inputs produced on the farm, caused by the decline in the relative price of the purchased inputs and the enhanced productivity which results from their use. For example, tractors have replaced horses, chemical fertilizer has substituted for farm manure, and farmers use proportionately less seeds

Table 5
Changes in the Pattern of Expenditure on Inputs for Selected
Years, 1938/9–1966/7, U.K.

Resource category	Pre-war	War-time	Post-war	Food ration-ing	Post-war	Post-rationing	
	1938/9	1943/4	1946/7	1951/2	1956/7	1961/2	1966/7
Feed	27·8	7·8	7·1	21·6	29·8	28·6	30·2
Labour	26·8	39·0	43·4	30·2	24·4	22·3	19·9
Rent and interest	17·8	11·7	10·4	7·8	7·0	8·7	10·3
Machinery	9·5	16·5	17·2	19·7	16·7	16·4	16·0
Fertilizer	3·9	7·7	6·4	6·6	8·0	9·0	8·3
Other	14·2	17·3	15·5	14·1	14·1	15·0	15·3
Total	100	100	100	100	100	100	100

Source: Ministry of Agriculture (1968), p. 78.

produced on their own farms.[1] As the tables only use broad
aggregate figures they mask the more extreme recent changes
such as the growth in the use of feed additives and pesticides.

When the changes in input use are netted out it can be shown
that the capital–labour ratio has increased substantially: in the
U.S., for example, the value of capital per worker increased
nearly sevenfold over the period 1940–60. For this reason it is
misleading to compare the performance of agriculture with
other industries in terms of the growth in their respective labour
productivities, when, in fact, growth of output depends upon
the changes in the use and mix of all inputs. The changing
pattern of resource use deserves attention in more detail.

We begin with the agricultural labour market. This has had
to adjust to the greatly increased use of capital. The labour
market deserves special attention because it is concerned with
men and women and because of the emphasis usually placed
on returns to labour rather than on returns to all factors. The

1. It can be seen then that for poor countries the ability of agriculture
to purchase inputs from other industries will help the emergence of a
multi-industry economy. This is analysed more fully in chapter 4.

following two sections view the influences on the demand for
tractors and fertilizer. A good understanding of the economic
variables influencing these factor markets will allow the student
to set up his own models of the factor markets, such as land,
feedstuffs and farm machinery, not analysed here.

The Agricultural Labour Market

A widely canvassed method of solving the problem of low farm
incomes is to adjust or decrease the size of the agricultural
labour force. This calls for a knowledge of the factors which
influence migration out of agriculture.

In this section we first set up a simple model of the hired
agricultural labour market and then examine how the variables
of the model combine to influence off-farm migration. We
conclude the section with an examination of the efficiency of
the labour market. A number of reasons are advanced as to
why, despite the extremely large labour transfer out of agriculture, the incomes of those employed in the agricultural sector
still lag behind those in other sectors. Policy implications are
presented at all stages.

A model of the hired agricultural labour market

Equations 3–5 below present a simple model of the hired agricultural labour market:

$$S_a = f_1 \left(\frac{W_a}{W_i}; U_i; \dot{U}_i; A; E \right) \qquad 3$$

$$D_a = f_2 \left(\frac{W_a}{P_k}; \frac{W_a}{P_a} \right) \qquad 4$$

$$S_a = D_a \qquad 5$$

Equation 3 indicates that the supply of labour to the agricultural
sector S_a is a function of first the relative wage rates in agriculture and industry (W_a/W_i), and, second, of the employment
opportunities in the non-agricultural sector, as indicated by the
industrial unemployment rate (U_i). Thus we would expect that

a rise in agricultural wage rates relative to industrial wages would increase the supply of labour to agriculture compared with what it otherwise would have been, and a fall in industrial unemployment would decrease the supply of labour to agriculture, it being easier to obtain employment in the non-farm sector. The third variable hypothesized to influence the supply of labour to agriculture is the change in industrial unemployment ($\dot{U}$). If it is rising rapidly then labour will tend to back-up on the farm, or even move back from industrial to agricultural employment. The remaining variables hypothesized to influence the agricultural labour supply are the age structure and educational attainment of the labour force.

Equation 4 explains the demand for labour in terms of the price ratio between labour and labour substitutes in agricultural production (W_a/P_k) and the real price of aggregate agricultural output (W_a/P_a) which determines the planned level of output. We would expect that the more expensive labour becomes relative to labour substitutes such as tractors, the lower the demand of the agricultural industry for labour, and the higher the agricultural product price the higher the planned output and the greater the demand for labour.

Equation 5 indicates the labour market is in equilibrium with the supply of labour to agriculture equal to the demand for labour by the industry. A more realistic dis-equilibrium model would allow for the existence of a disparity between demand and supply which would establish for the hired labour market a dynamic wage adjustment process.

$$\dot{W}_a = f_3 \; [\, (S_a - D_a); Z \,] \qquad\qquad 6$$

Equation 6 indicates then that the rate of change of money wages in agriculture ($\dot{W}_a$) is determined by the excess demand for labour in agriculture (whether positive or negative) which is usually expressed as percentage unemployment, and a set of relevant exogenous variables, Z, such as changes in the cost of living and changes in the level of the profits of agriculture.[1]

1. This simple model, therefore, shows at the industry level the basis of the Phillips curve, which attempts to explain changes in money wage rates as a function of unemployment. For details of this relationship for agriculture see Cowling and Metcalf (1965).

Labour migration from agriculture[1]

In recent years the dynamic adjustment of the labour demand and supply factors, presented in the model above, has consistently produced a lower level of employment in agriculture. Details of the number of agricultural workers are given in Table 6. The decline in numbers may be realized in three ways – migration, unemployment and the recruitment–retirement balance. We are here only concerned with the first component.

In Britain, the vast bulk of the migrants are hired regular whole-time workers, whose number fell by more than half over the post-war period, from 739,000 in 1946 to 342,000 in 1966 (Table 6). Statistics of the number of farmers are not published, but are estimated currently to number around 220,000. Numbers of farmers are thought to have fallen very slightly over the post-war period. Similarly, the number of part-time and seasonal-casual workers has fallen only slightly from the 1946 figure of 150,000 to 146,000 in 1966.

In the U.S.A., by contrast, the greater proportion of the reduction in the agricultural labour force is accounted for by the reduction in the number of family workers (who also form the bulk of the total farm workforce). Between 1940 and 1960 the total agricultural labour force fell from eleven million to just over seven million, three million of this reduction comprising family workers.

The consequences of this out-migration may be examined from many angles. In the U.K. the fact that the large majority of labour transfer is hired labour is likely to have, in time, far-reaching effects on the over-all farm structure, tending to produce in Britain the family farm set-up found in the U.S.A. and many European countries. This may, in the long run, reduce the flexibility of the industry as farm families tend to be much less mobile than hired workers. On the industrial side,

1. The term migration in this context refers to people switching their jobs from agriculture to some other undefined sector of the economy and need not involve migration in the geographical sense in that it may be possible for a farm worker to stay in the same house or area, even after changing jobs.

Table 6
Numbers of Agricultural Workers in Great Britain (in thousands)

Year	Total	Regular whole-time	Part-time	Seasonal and casual
1921	996	789	207	
1931	829	714	115	
1941	759	602	157	
1946	889	739	150	
1947	891	739	153	
1948	849	682	168	
1949	855	685	171	
1950	843	670	172	
1951	812	642	171	
1952	804	618	186	
1953	780	600	179	
1954	755	583	172	
1955	732	554	86	91
1956	700	528	83	90
1957	696	520	86	90
1958	679	503	80	96
1959	669	493	79	97
1960	645	473	80	92
1961	617	449	71	97
1962	589	430	67	92
1963	569	416	66	87
1964	544	389	67	88
1965	514	365	64	86
1966	488	342	60	86

Source: Ministry of Agriculture (1968), p. 62.

migration from the farm provides a continuous source of labour for the other sectors of the economy.[1]

1. This release of labour is designated the 'factor' contribution of agriculture to economic growth: see chapter 4. The importance of this source of labour in aiding economic growth was explicitly recognized in the U.K. *National Plan* (Cmnd 2764, H.M.S.O., 1965), where it was stated that it was thought that agriculture would continue to release substantial manpower resources, over 20,000 p.a., and so help in closing the 'manpower gap' expected during the plan period 1966–70.

Both supply and demand factors have influenced the transfer of labour from agriculture. The supply factors are those which 'pull' labour from agriculture and the demand variables are those which 'push' labour from that sector. We concentrate here on explaining the influence of those variables of an economic nature, although it is recognized that socio-economic variables such as poor housing, irregular hours and lack of promotion prospects will certainly have an influence on migration. Among the main economic variables, at both national and regional level, are the following, all but one being pull (supply) variables.[1]

The level of industrial unemployment. An historical relationship has been observed between the rate of off-farm migration and the business cycle, migration being greater when the level of unemployment in the non-agricultural sector falls. In the depression of the inter-war period the high levels of unemployment in the industrial sector of the U.S.A. caused labour to back up on the farm and resulted in negative migration – an absolute increase in the farm labour force. The off-farm opportunities are best reflected in the level of unemployment and vacancies in industries to which agricultural migrants move, such as construction and services, rather than the over-all level of industrial unemployment.

The change in industrial unemployment. The change in the industrial unemployment level (a rise in the level from 2 per cent to 3 per cent, being a 50 per cent change) is likely to influence the *expectations* of migrants. Thus if unemployment is rising, even if the level is low, this will act as a brake on migration as potential migrants will expect more difficulty in finding alternative employment and postpone or abandon their intention to move. This brake on migration will be heightened

1. The variables are drawn from a study which was concerned to explain migration of hired male agricultural workers, but generally these same factors would influence the extent of migration amongst farmers and farm families. See Cowling and Metcalf (1968). This article refers to a number of studies of off-farm migration and the references will not be repeated here.

if 'last hired, first fired' agreements are in operation in those industries to which migrants move.

Analyses of migration at a regional level suggest that in regions which have persistent high unemployment levels migrants are less likely to be influenced by changes in their own regional unemployment level than are agricultural workers in regions of low industrial unemployment. This probably reflects the fact that agricultural workers in high-unemployment regions are likely to move further afield than those in low-unemployment regions, and therefore the relevant indicator of alternative employment opportunities is, for them, the level and change in national unemployment rather than that in their own region.

Industrialization and proximity to alternative employment. At a regional level the higher the local level of industrialization the greater the pull that is exercised. A measure of regional industrialization might be calculated as the ratio of agricultural to total employees, the lower the ratio the greater the degree of industrialization. The effect of a high degree of industrialization on migration will be accentuated by the fact that the greater the density of non-farm activities the less distance potential migrants should have to travel to find a new place of employment.

Ratio of agricultural to industrial earnings. Generally we would expect and typically find a negative relationship between these two variables, the higher the ratio of agricultural earnings to industrial earnings in those sectors to which agricultural workers move, the lower the likely rate of migration. An exception to this was a U.S. study (Bishop, 1961) which found that migration increased as the wage ratio rose and the author interpreted this by suggesting that the increased agricultural earnings provided the capital necessary for migration. The amount of funds necessary to transfer from agriculture will be greater the longer the time period the migrant might have to wait to get an alternative job and the farther he has to move; therefore lack of capital is unlikely to be as important in the U.K. as in the U.S.A., as the prevailing industrial unemployment level is lower in the U.K. and migrants generally have to move shorter distances.

Ratio of agricultural wage earnings to agricultural product prices. As unit labour costs rise relative to product prices, the farmer has an incentive either to substitute capital for labour (assuming that the price of capital does not rise so rapidly as that of labour) and/or to reduce planned output. In either case the result is a *push* of hired labour from the land. Increases in the guaranteed prices of agricultural products which raise farm income hinder migration and maintain a larger number of people in agriculture than would otherwise be there.

Age and education. The lower the average age and the higher the level of educational attainment of agricultural labour, the higher the likely rate of off-farm migration, as it is likely that the earnings and employment potential outside agriculture is greater for better educated, younger migrants. This positive relationship is likely to be accentuated because the better educated the employee the more aware and concerned he is likely to be about prospects in industry.

Whilst different studies produce somewhat different results as to the relative importance of these variables in explaining labour transfer from agriculture, the consensus which has emerged as to their respective influences does allow us to draw some tentative policy implications. First, most studies confirm the influence of the level and change of industrial unemployment in influencing migration. Given that the authorities will continue to manipulate the internal level of aggregate demand (and therefore unemployment) this implies that the numbers migrating from agriculture will not be steady, but rather will be cyclical, inversely related to unemployment. Second, the ratio of agricultural earnings to industrial earnings appears to have a significant effect on migration. Therefore, a deliberate policy of raising the pay of lower paid workers, who most certainly include agricultural workers, relative to other workers, which is an avowed aim of both the U.S. and U.K. governments, will result in a reduction in the outflow compared with what it otherwise would be. A further important point concerning the policy implications of relative earnings arises from the relationship of industrial earnings to industrial unemployment. Estimates have suggested that if unemployment rises 1 per cent the rate of earnings inflation is reduced by the order of 3 per cent. It is highly likely therefore that a rise in unemployment will not only induce a reduction of migration by itself, but will also reduce the relative advance of industrial earnings and thus cause a further decline in the percentage outflow.

Third, the evidence suggests that agricultural price supports result in the retention of more resources in agriculture than would otherwise be the case. A probably minor inducement to migration can be achieved by a reduction in agricultural price support, or a restructuring of subsidies away from relatively labour-intensive crops. It is possible that the push from the land might result in agricultural unemployment, either before or as well as migration and job transfer. This would reduce agricultural earnings and accentuate the pull of the earnings ratio.

The evidence on the remaining variables is somewhat conflicting and inconclusive, therefore the policy implications as to the effects on migration of these variables awaits further research.

The efficiency of the labour market

Broadly, the criterion of efficiency in the labour market is that labour of equivalent capacities should earn the same real marginal return in all employment. Now, despite the persistent large outflow of labour from agriculture, the earnings of agricultural workers remain significantly below those of industrial employees. Does this indicate that the labour market is operating inefficiently or does it suggest that the quality of the agricultural workers is in some sense, physical or mental, lower than that of industrial workers?[1]

1. Among other causes of lower agricultural earnings is the possibility that the retail price level is lower in rural areas. However, this would account for only very little of the discrepancy between earnings in the farm and non-farm sectors.

The imperfections in the labour market might occur through lack of information about non-farm employment prospects and industrial unemployment impeding the extent of off-farm migration. If such imperfections are the cause of the earnings differential and could be rectified, it would follow that a substantial part of the agricultural labour force, given their existing quality (skills and abilities) would earn more if employed in the industrial sector.

The alternative explanation of the persistence in the earnings differential is that potential earnings of migrants are related to their agricultural earnings and the numbers on the farm reflect the fact that agricultural workers may in fact be earning as much or more in their present farm occupation than they would in alternative jobs. If this explanation is true then it follows that the usual postulated cure for the low agricultural incomes, namely a more rapid exodus of labour from agriculture, may not necessarily level up earnings in agriculture to the prevailing levels in non-farm sectors.

Evidence suggests that both of these hypotheses have a part in explaining the lower agricultural incomes. One recent study (Hathaway and Perkins, 1968), however, suggests that for the U.S.A. the labour market is working efficiently and that the agricultural income problem may well be intractable. It found that nearly a half of the persons changing from farm to non-farm employment over 1957–60 sustained a *loss* in earnings and that the average of gains was surprisingly low. This study also suggests that, for the U.S.A. anyway, lack of information does not inhibit labour mobility as the net outflow is composed of both off-farm and in-farm (i.e. labour moving from non-agricultural sectors to agriculture) movements in the ratio of 10:9, thus gross movements were nineteen times as large as net movements.

However, similar facts possibly may not hold with such force for European countries, where factors such as ignorance of opportunities, a fear of urban life, personal ties and trade union restrictions may all be at work to inhibit off-farm mobility; also, of course, it may simply be that many farm workers possess alternative objective functions to that of earnings maximization, being prepared to sacrifice income for the privilege of living in a rural area.

Overall, then, it remains true that to eliminate the gap between agricultural and industrial incomes it is necessary to encourage resource mobility, but more recent studies indicate that there may come some point where workers in agriculture, although earning less than workers in the non-farm sector, are getting higher returns than they would if they moved to the industrial sector, in which case agricultural incomes can then only be raised by other means such as direct exchequer subsidization.

Demand for Durable Inputs

Economic growth is associated with a substitution of capital for labour. This has most certainly been observed in agriculture where the number and value of durable inputs has increased greatly whilst the labour input has declined.

Table 7 shows the growth in the numbers of certain types of agricultural machinery in Great Britain since 1942. These statistics understate the services which flow from the stock of durable inputs as their quality has been improved substantially through time.

We now turn, then, to an examination of the factors which we would expect to be important in explaining the large investment in durable inputs undertaken by the agricultural sector. Farm buildings are taken to represent durable inputs as a whole. The underlying theory applies equally, however, to specifying the investment function for other durable inputs such as tractors and milking machines. The following factors are important.

Existing stocks

The demand for gross annual investment in farm buildings comes from two sources. First, the need to replace existing buildings because of capital consumption (depreciation). The greater the stock of farm buildings, the greater the absolute amount of depreciation and the higher is the replacement demand. Second, the desire to increase the stock of buildings to

Table 7

Estimated Numbers of Certain Types of Agricultural Machinery in Great Britain

Year	Tractors	Combine harvesters	Milking machine installations
1942	116,830	1,000	29,510
1944	n.a.	2,500	37,790
1946	204,322	3,464	48,286
1948	261,180	5,225	n.a.
1950	332,206	10,470	78,753
1952	367,099	17,255	90,963
1954	438,888	22,362	101,615
1956	477,809	32,896	n.a.
1959	474,984	51,735	n.a.
1961	480,743	54,243	120,140
1964	495,751	62,038	n.a.

n.a.: not available.
Source: Ministry of Agriculture (1968), pp. 71–3.

the level indicated by the values of the decision variables. Greater stocks of farm buildings decrease the marginal product of the flow of services accruing from the stock. The existing stock of buildings thus has a dampening influence on the investment. Therefore the two sources from which the investment demand is derived pull in opposite directions. We are here concerned with the latter problem: namely to indicate the variables which influence the farmers' desire to increase or decrease the stock of farm buildings, and these are indicated below.

Net farm income

Net farm income (gross receipts less production expenses) is similar to profits. The level of income is likely to affect investment for two reasons. Theoretically a durable asset should be purchased if the present value of the discounted stream of future earnings from the asset is greater than the price of the asset.[1] Past levels of net farm income are likely to figure largely in farmers' expectations about future income and therefore in their expectations of the future stream of earnings resulting from the asset. Second, the decision to invest in a durable asset will be influenced by the farmer's ability to pay for it. If past farm incomes have been high, a farmer is more likely to be able to purchase it, or at least pay the minimum required deposit. Also his assessment of his ability to meet future mortgage commitments will depend on his expectations as to net farm income. These are likely to be based, partly at least, on past levels. Similarly, if he wishes to borrow to purchase the asset, the financial institution lending the money will probably be more interested in his ability to repay the loan than in the rate of return on the asset. The rate of return might be highly variable. This would affect the farmer's ability to repay the loan in regular instalments. Therefore, past levels of net farm income affect both internal (the farmer's) and external (the institution's) expectations about his ability to repay the loan.

Both ability to pay and expectations are influenced by past levels of net farm income. Therefore in specifying the investment function a weighted average of net farm income should be included as the relevant variable. For example, where Y = net farm income and t = years, the weights might be

$$\frac{3Y_{t-1} + 2Y_{t-2} + 1Y_{t-3}}{6}.$$

1. This assumes that the objective of the firm is to maximize profits. Whilst it is recognized that this may well be an unreasonable assumption of the objectives of firms comprising some industries, who may be concerned with some other objective such as sales maximization, it remains a reasonable assumption of the objective function of firms in agriculture. The market structure of the agricultural sector approximates to perfect competition. Under this structure firms must maximize profits (minimize costs), or accept a rate of return below that gained by the profit maximizers and ultimately probably leave the industry.

Prices

The price of an input relative both to the prices of other inputs and to the price of the output is likely to influence the demand for the input. The importance of the ratio of farm building prices to the prices of other inputs, whether substitutes or complements, stems from marginal theory. As the relative input prices change this induces a change in the input mix. The ratio of farm building prices to the product prices received by farmers is a relevant variable in the investment function because the product prices received by farmers are likely to have an important influence on their expectations as to future product prices. These in turn influence expected farm incomes. A programme of guaranteed farm product prices coupled with long term guarantees as to their level is likely to have a favourable influence on expectations as to future product prices, and therefore incomes and investment.

The accelerator

The accelerator relates investment to the change in output. It assumes a prescribed capital–output ratio. If farmers increase their output the accelerator principle assumes that they then invest to increase their capital stock to maintain the capital–output ratio. In fact it is very difficult to isolate the causal relationship. The value of output may increase because of investment in the capital inputs. Or, farmers may invest in the durable inputs to maintain the capital–output ratio. If it is thought that investment in farm buildings does depend on output, then the investment function should include a variable to represent output. One possibility would be to deflate the index of gross farm income by an index of product prices received by farmers, giving in some sense a measure of aggregate farm output.

Monetary variables

Classically, the rate of interest was thought to be the main determinant of investment. Theoretically the farmer should invest in a durable input if the rate of return on that investment is greater than the rate of interest. However, studies both of aggregate investment and investment in agriculture cast doubt on the importance of the rate of interest as a determinant of investment (Meyer and Kuh, 1957, p. 8; Cromarty, 1959).

This may be because the rate of return on capital in agriculture varies widely because of exogenous factors such as weather. Therefore ability-to-pay considerations may be more important than the rate of return on capital. Nevertheless, the interest rate is likely to be important in explaining investment if it acts as a proxy variable (that is, if it represents the availability of funds). Evidence does suggest that an inverse correlation exists between these two financial variables (Gehrels and Wiggins, 1957). An increase in the supply of funds to potential borrowers is associated with a decrease in the rate of interest. Therefore, when the interest rate falls, investment is likely to rise both because it becomes cheaper to borrow funds and because the supply of these funds increases.

Fiscal variables

The government does much to encourage capital formation. The estimated cost of support to U.K. agriculture in recent years with respect to agricultural buildings and works is given in Table 8. It will be noted that the two major costs have been subsidies towards farm improvements and field drainage. These subsidies do not normally cover the whole cost of the investment in the capital equipment, and must be viewed partially as catalysts which encourage investment. For example, between 1960 and 1964 total capital investment in projects covered by the Farm Improvement Scheme was £83·9 million, the cost of the subsidy being £37·5 million. Similarly, fixed capital formation in drainage was valued at £20·1 million of which £8·3 million was met by the exchequer.

Gross fixed capital formation in agriculture, as in the rest of the economy, has been encouraged during the post-war period by investment allowances, which enabled firms to offset a certain percentage of the cost of a new machine or building against profits for taxation purposes. This system was replaced in 1967 by a system of cash grants which cover a certain

proportion of the cost of the investment. In agriculture the
government provides a grant of one tenth of the cost of all fixed
equipment.[1] The cost to the exchequer of these investment
incentives will be around £10 million in 1968/9.

Table 8
Cost of Exchequer Support on Selected Capital Items (£ million)

Year ending: Item	1960	1961	1962	1963	1964	1965	1966	1967	1968	1969
Field drainage	2·6	2·7	2·7	3·0	2·6	3·1	3·1	3·2	4·0	4·5
Water supply	0·7	0·8	0·8	0·8	0·7	0·7	0·6	0·5	0·5	0·5
Farm improvements	6·6	7·8	9·2	10·3	10·2	11·5	11·6	11·1	12·3	13·2
Investment grants	—	—	—	—	—	—	—	—	7·0	9·5
Silos	1·4	0·9	0·8	0·6	0·3	0·3	0·2	0·2	0·1	—

Source: Cmnd. 3558, *Annual Review and Determination of Guarantees*,
H.M.S.O., 1968.

Farm size and other technical factors

Average farm size is increasing through time through amalgamation and consolidation of holdings. This can have either a
favourable or dampening effect on investment in farm buildings.
The structural adjustment might cause an increase in the demand for new buildings through a desire to make the enlarged
farm technically up to date. Alternatively, it could result in a
discouragement of new investment as the existing building
capacity could be more fully utilized.

Another technical factor which might influence the demand
for farm buildings is a shift in the relative proportions of agricultural products produced. For example, a rise in the relative

1. Increased temporarily during 1967 and 1968 to 12½ per cent.

price of beef and milk might encourage farmers to switch out of cash crops and into livestock production. This would result in an increase in the demand for farm building investment because of the greater shelter and feedlot needs of livestock and the enhanced requirements for storing feedingstuffs. (Incidentally, it would result in a simultaneous decrease in the demand for farm tractor services.) This output ratio could be specified in the investment function as the ratio of livestock income to total farm income. The higher this ratio the higher the likely demand for farm buildings.

Improved quality and improved knowledge

Durable agricultural inputs have been subject to substantial quality changes through time. This quality improvement increases the marginal physical productivity of the input which will lead to an increase in the demand for the input. Similarly, the demand function will also be shifted outwards through time because of the greater technical knowledge of farmers.

Prestige

The farmer may increase his satisfaction, though not necessarily his profits, by buying a new building, or replacing an old one, earlier than the date indicated by economic criteria. He may therefore view the building as a consumer good rather than as a capital good. This prestige motive for investment may be accentuated by the fact that the possession of the new building may enhance utility by increasing the farmer's leisure time. These factors are all likely to lead to a level of machinery investment greater than the economic optimum.

Demand for Chemical Fertilizer.[1]

There exist three main forms of chemical fertilizer nutrients: nitrogen (N), phosphate (P_2O_5) and potash (K_2O). These nutrients may be applied as parts of a compound, or in the case of N and P_2O_5 may be applied straight. To estimate the

1. See also Metcalf and Cowling (1967). This study contains references to the important U.S. literature on fertilizer demand functions and these will not be repeated here.

growth in the usage of fertilizer it is necessary to measure not simply the tonnage applied to the soil but the plant food nutrients concentrated into this tonnage. Thus if the concentration level of fertilizers is going up it is possible to have an increase in tonnage consumption of plant nutrients whilst applying a stable or declining tonnage.

The growth in the use of chemical fertilizer has been spectacular in the post-war period. For example, Table 9 shows that U.K. consumption of plant nutrients went up from 628,000 tons in 1946/7 to 1,581,000 tons in 1966/7, an increase of over 150 per cent. The table also indicates that the relative use of nitrogen has increased substantially, from a little over a quarter of the total in 1946/7 to over two-fifths in 1966/7. This reflects both a heavier application of nitrogen on crops and a wider use on grassland.

Table 9
Fertilizer Use in the U.K.

Year	Nitrogen		Phosphates		Potash		Total	
	1000 nutrient tons	Per cent of total	1000 nutrient tons	Per cent of total	1000 nutrient tons	Per cent of total	1000 nutrient tons	Per cent of total
1946/7	164	26·1	357	56·8	107	17·0	628	100
1951/2	181	28·0	277	43·5	172	27·3	630	100
1956/7	286	29·5	374	38·5	309	31·8	969	100
1961/2	494	34·8	485	34·1	442	31·1	1421	100
1962/3	495	37·2	437	32·9	397	29·9	1329	100
1963/4	554	37·8	477	32·6	434	29·6	1465	100
1964/5	565	38·3	479	32·4	433	29·3	1477	100
1965/6	589	40·2	435	29·7	440	30·1	1464	100
1966/7	685	43·3	459	29·0	437	27·6	1581	100

Source: Ministry of Agriculture, *Statistics* 27 (Annual).

In view of the large rise in use, and the importance of fertilizer in the process of agricultural development in poor countries, it is necessary to try to isolate the factors responsible for the growth in demand for chemical fertilizer. Empirical studies suggest the following are important explanatory variables.

Real price of fertilizer

Studies have generally found the price of fertilizer deflated by either crop prices or by an index of all agricultural product prices to be an important influence on fertilizer usage, a decline in the price of fertilizer relative to the price of agricultural products encouraging greater application of fertilizer. Consider Figure 5: the production function indicates output per unit of fertilizer input. The optimum demand for fertilizer depends on the slope of the price line (fertilizer price deflated by agricultural product price to give the real price of fertilizer); thus if fertilizer becomes cheaper relative to agricultural product prices, the slope flattens and it pays the farmer to move along the production function and apply more fertilizer.

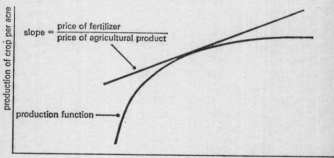

Figure 5   Relationship between yield, price and rate of fertilizer application

Farm income

A higher farm income is likely to lead to increased use of fertilizer. A higher income improves the liquidity position and the availability of funds for the purchase of fertilizer by the farmer. Under conditions of limited operating capital farmers may be unable to fertilize at optimal rates. Thus, assuming that at any one time farmers are applying nutrients at a sub-optimal rate a higher level of income will help them achieve the optimum application. There is considerable evidence in the U.K. that nitrogen is being applied at sub-optimal levels, especially on grassland.

Improved knowledge

An upward shift in the demand function for fertilizers occurs through time because of the greater technological knowledge of farmers, resulting from their own findings, education, sales programmes and extension services. The diffusion of knowledge and acceptance of chemical fertilizers occurred, for advanced countries, initially in arable areas and is presently continuing on grassland. In addition, farmers have, through time, adopted better varieties of seeds, and the increased use of fertilizers is frequently a necessary complement to these improved seed varieties.

Prices of other inputs

A positive relationship exists between use of plant nutrients and the real price of feedstuffs. There are two reasons for this. Firstly, one of the features of fertilizer usage has been the increasing application to grassland. Fertilizer may thus be considered a substitute for purchased feed; if the price of feedstuffs rises relative to the price of fertilizer, this will induce farmers to apply more fertilizer to grassland and reduce the amount of bought feedstuffs necessary for livestock. This holds especially for nitrogen which is the most important fertilizer input applied to grassland. Secondly, if the price of feedstuffs rises this may induce farmers to increase fertilizer application to those crops used for animal feed, inducing higher yield and enabling farmers to either sell these feedgrains at the higher price or to use them on their own farms.

Fertilizer consumption may also be affected by the price of other inputs. U.S. studies have indicated a substitute relationship exists between fertilizer consumption and the price of

land. Again, there exists the possibility that labour is a complement to fertilizer in that there exists a technical relationship
between application of fertilizer and required labour input, but
it is unlikely that farmers would cut down on their use of
fertilizer because of an increase in the price of labour.

The fact that the above variables appear to be important in
determining fertilizer consumption enables certain policy implications to be drawn. Fertilizer consumption is responsive to
changes in the real price of fertilizer and thus an upward adjustment in prices will cause fertilizer consumption to fall below
what it otherwise would be.

Such an upward adjustment in the real price of fertilizers
might come about if the government reduces the guaranteed
prices of the agricultural products, or if the fertilizer manufacturers raise prices, say because of a rise in the world prices
of the chemical inputs. In the U.K. the government subsidizes
fertilizer consumption, making the net cost to the farmer less
than the true market price; a withdrawal of this subsidy would
raise the real price. However, whilst the price response has been
demonstrated studies have also shown that a strong upward
trend in consumption exists associated with the diffusion of the
new fertilizer technology through agriculture. Price adjustments are made around this upward trend causing year-to-year
variations in consumption. It is likely that the propelling force
behind the trend has undergone some structural change
through time. Initially it represented the diffusion of fertilizer
technology among cash-crop producers and then more recently,
as crop producers have attained optimal usage, this has been
superseded by the diffusion among livestock producers for use
on grassland. Finally, higher farm income and improved
liquidity will encourage fertilizer consumption, especially
nitrogen.

3 Technical Change and Innovation

Introduction

The agricultural problems of high-income countries are very different from those of low-income countries. In many high-income countries, especially the U.S.A., a major agricultural policy problem is that of surplus production. In contrast, in low-income countries the crucial problem is that of scarcity, with food production hardly able to keep pace with population growth. The rapid adoption and diffusion of innovations is an important explanatory factor accounting for farm surpluses. Lack of suitable inventions and the failure of relevant inventions to be widely diffused are important in explaining farm scarcity problems in poor countries. Each of these problems will be analysed in more detail in chapters 7 and 4 respectively. In this chapter we are concerned with technical change itself. First we review the interaction between technical change and economic growth, and then consider the process of diffusion and adoption of innovations.

Technology refers to the *stock* of techniques, procedures or ways of ordering economic activity, whereas technical change occurs with the *addition* of a *new* production technique to the existing stock of technology. A firm can change its production technique either by adopting the new technology or changing its input mix within the constraint imposed by existing technology. Consider Figure 6. First the production technique can change through technical change. If, for example, the farmer adopts a new improved variety of seeds then with the same intake of all other factors as previously the input of new variety seed, Oa, increases output by bc; that is, the prod-

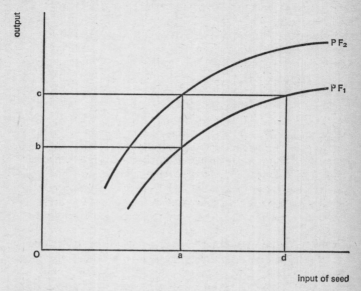

Figure 6 Changes in production technique

uction function has been shifted upwards.[1] Alternatively, the firm could change its production technique and increase its output, by keeping within the bounds of the existing original technology and moving along the original production function PF_1; by employing ad more of the original variety of seed, in combination with the same quantities of other factors,

1. It must be emphasized here that if the production function were specified correctly, i.e. the original seed varieties being replaced in the production function by new varieties, then the x axis of Figure 6 would not itself remain the same. However, the above describes the concept of technical change adequately: the same quantity of an improved input resulting in higher output with the intake if other factors held constant. The problem of the correct specification of the production function is discussed, for the aggregate industry level, in the next section.

output can similarly be increased by bc. For example, assume the seed-producing industry itself experiences technical change, i.e. an upward shift in its production function, and it now becomes cheaper to produce a given seed output of the original seed type, and that this is reflected in a lower seed price to the farmer; the farmer will now alter his combination of inputs, using more seed, and possibly substituting seed for other inputs. Thus whilst the underlying farm production function has remained unchanged (i.e. there has been no technical change to the farmer), the individual farm has increased output by bc by changing the production technique, i.e. moving along the original production function PF_1 and increasing seed input by ad. In this case, therefore, the increased output has resulted not from technical change in the agricultural input–output relationship, but rather through a change in market conditions reflected through the factor supply and demand schedules.

It can be seen then that the economic impact of technical change percolates through three stages. Initially it has an impact on the cost structure or product mix inside the *farm-firms* which take up the new technology. Second, this in turn leads to a shift in the *industry* demand schedules for inputs and supply schedules for final products; third, this in turn allows a higher G.N.P. or more leisure for the whole working population.

The Input–Output Ratio

It has been increasingly realized that the serious agricultural adjustment problem of advanced countries is one of input and output magnitudes. Output has been large in relation to demand and the resources retained in the industry have been large relative to the income available for distribution, thus factor returns, especially to labour, have been low compared with other industries. In this section we briefly explore the changes in the aggregate agricultural input–output ratio, which, conventionally measured, has declined significantly through time.[1] What are the reasons for this increase in the ratio of output to input?

Studies using the concept of the aggregate agricultural production function, that is, an industry level production function, offer some guidance. The earliest studies related the increasing output to the raw inputs of the quantities of land, labour and capital (and other conventional inputs) used. The studies, however, left varying amounts of the output increase unexplained. This unexplained element is termed the *residual* and is generally attributable to one or other of the nebulous ghost factors of 'technological change' and enhanced managerial skill.

More recent studies, using more sophisticated measures of the inputs, have reduced the residual (Griliches, 1960 and 1963). First, they take account of the improved *quality of the capital*; for example, instead of using the number of tractors as a relevant capital input, a composite measure could be developed taking into account, in addition to quantity, qualitative features such as horse-power, engine type, steel quality, whether they protect the operator from bad weather, etc., all of which increase the productivity of the farm tractors. Second, the measurement of the labour input now takes account not only of the man-hours worked, but also of the *quality of the human agent*, a strong positive relation existing between the level of skills and knowledge of farm operators and farm workers and their productivity. For example, the labour input may be adjusted for the increasing number of years spent in education by agricultural workers; through time, therefore, the agricultural workforce has received an increasing amount of education. Third, it has been suggested that part of the previously unexplained element is attributable to the increasing size of

1. For example, in the agricultural sector of the U.S.A. over the period 1910–50, inputs increased between 14 and 33 per cent (land and capital use increasing and labour use decreasing) and output rose by 75 per cent. See Schultz (1953), pp. 108–9. For the U.K., over the period 1948–62, agricultural output increased by 2·6 per cent per annum, whilst the factor input *declined* by 0·2 per cent per annum. The residual growth, therefore, equals 2·8 per cent per annum. See Matthews (1964).

holdings, which resulted in substantial *economies of scale* and in a trend towards *increasing specialization*. Fourth, the inclusion of agricultural *research and development expenditure* as an input in the aggregate production function reduced the unexplained residual element.

It can be seen then that the unexplained or residual element in the growth of agricultural output is essentially a measure of our ignorance of some of the causes of this output increase, which is cloaked by calling it technical change. The more correctly the factors of production are specified – accounting for such things as quality improvements in the capital inputs, increasing concentration of plant nutrients in fertilizer, improved feed additives and the enhanced skills and knowledge of the farm population – the less of the increasing output–input ratio needs to be attributed to improvements in technology, know-how and entrepreneurship. However, in order that these new or improved inputs contribute substantially to the explanation of the increase in agricultural output they have to be widely diffused, and it is to the process of the diffusion of agricultural innovations that we now turn.

The Diffusion of Innovations

In this section the diffusion and adoption of innovation in agriculture is analysed. We shall describe the process of diffusion and discuss some of the factors which are responsible for some farmers adopting innovations before others.

An innovation may be defined as 'any thought, behaviour or thing that is new because it is qualitatively different from existing forms'. An innovation encompasses both the discovery *and application* of a new idea to a product, method or organization, whilst an invention is only the first stage in the process of innovation – an invention has to be developed and applied to become an innovation. Innovations may be classified according to the changes they make. For agriculture and related industries these are broadly of two sorts, each innovation having one or both of these effects.[1] First, an innovation may leave the final product unchanged but reduce the unit cost of the output; these innovations tend to result in increased total output.[2] The second type of innovation is the provision of new products or services. The innovation of chemical fertilizer thus involved both these changes in that it was a new product, replacing the traditional organic fertilizer, but it also had the effect of reducing unit costs and increasing the total output of agricultural products, which remained qualitatively unchanged by the new fertilizer form.

We must distinguish between diffusion and adoption. *Diffusion* is concerned with the spread of innovations both between persons and geographical areas. In both the inter-personal and inter-area elements of diffusion there will be a time lag between those persons or areas which take up the innovations early and the late acceptors of the innovation. *Adoption* is the last stage in accepting an innovation; typically an individual farmer will go through the following sequence in taking up the innovation: awareness – interest – evaluation – trial – adoption (Rogers, 1958). If the percentage of farmers adopting an innovation is plotted against the time of adoption, we usually attain the bell-shaped curve of Figure 7.

Whilst a few farmers will adopt the innovation rapidly, the bulk of producers will take more time to become aware of the new practice or idea and to evaluate the benefits of the innovation.[3] If over a range of different innovations a farmer is

1. There is also a third type of innovation consisting of changes in business organization or market structures. For example, the increasing reliance by farmers on contract selling and the growth of co-operatives and supermarkets are innovations in this sense. The motives for, and results of, these structural innovations are analysed more fully in chapter 6.

2. If, however, the farmer is more concerned to maximize his leisure, subject to a certain level of profits being achieved, these innovations will probably not lead to an increase in total output.

3. If the bell-shaped curve describing the diffusion process is assumed to be a normal curve, farmers can be classified according to their deviation from the mean time of adoption. Thus the majority of farmers adopt the innovation within the periods bounded by the mean time of

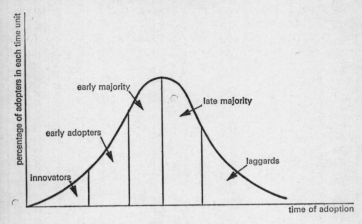

Figure 7 Classification of adopters by time of adoption

persistently among the first to adopt the new product or practice he can be classified as an innovator, and so on through the time scale to the other extreme, where, if he is consistently tardy in adopting each innovation, he is classified as a laggard.

We may determine the shape of the national curve of diffusion by replotting the bell-shaped curve of Figure 7 cumulatively which results in the S-shaped curve of Figure 8.

However, it is unlikely that each *region* will adopt the innovation at the same rate, partly because the innovation may not be available in all regions simultaneously. Thus in the curve of Figure 8 the national percentage of farmers adopting an innovation by time period $t + 2$ is 50 per cent. However, the more progressive areas may have achieved a 50 per cent adoption rate by time period $t + 1$ and the least progressive may take till $t + 3$. It can be seen then that both farmers within a group and regions within a country will probably adopt innovations

adoption $(x) \pm$ one standard deviation (σ); the innovators in the period prior to $x-2\sigma$; early adopters in the period between $x-2\sigma$ and $x-\sigma$; and laggards in the period after $x+\sigma$. See Rogers (1962).

at different speeds. Let us therefore suggest some of the factors which influence the speed of adoption.[1]

First, the *economic* attributes of the innovations: for example, we could hypothesize *a priori* that the lower the initial and

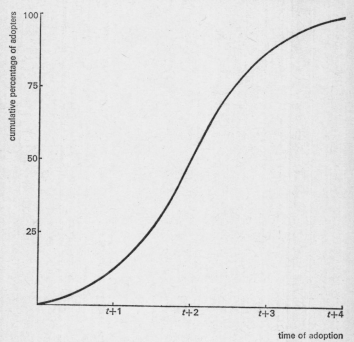

Figure 8 National curve of diffusion

operating costs and the larger the rate of return on the capital and effect on farm income, the more rapidly the innovation would be diffused. However, research findings conflict as to the

1. We concentrate here on factors present at the micro level, rather than national factors such as the level of investment grants and the extent of production subsidies in agriculture. For a fuller discussion of factors affecting the speed of diffusion of agricultural innovations see Jones (1963) on which this discussion is based.

validity of these assertions and this suggests that other variables are also relevant.

Second, the *technical* characteristics of the innovation: for example, if an innovation is complex and therefore difficult for the farmer to assimilate, the slower the likely rate of adoption. If the innovation is complex the farmer will be uncertain as to how much his costs will be lowered, or his income increased, if he adopts it. If the innovation is indivisible, as capital innovations will be, this does not permit the farmer the possibility of a controlled experiment to evaluate its worth; in contrast, farmers are able to compare new fertilizers, new breeds of cattle and new seed varieties with existing products, initially probably on a small scale, and this reduces the uncertainty surrounding the desirability or otherwise of adopting the innovation. Also, if an innovation is to be diffused rapidly, it will have to be compatible with the farmer's existing production techniques. Third, the *prestige* associated with the innovation may influence the speed of adoption. This may be especially important with conspicuous capital items such as combine harvesters.

Fourth, the *characteristics of the farmer* adopting the innovation: generally a farmer is likely to take up an innovation more rapidly the larger his farm, the higher his income and socio-economic status and the more educated he is; also older farmers tend to adopt new practices more slowly. Similarly, research suggests that if a farmer has certain 'urban attitudes' such as being raised in a town or availing himself of urban amenities, he is more likely to adopt innovations earlier than his completely rural-based neighbour. This may be because he pays attention to the technical journals and the agricultural advisory services, whilst the later adopters are more likely to rely, for their information, on the new practice of neighbouring farmers who have previously adopted the innovation.

Let us now turn to an example of the geographical aspect of diffusion. This is a study of the diffusion of the hybrid corn innovation in the U.S.A. (Griliches, 1957). It was found that the speed of diffusion varied substantially between states. There are three elements involved: the year by which a certain minimum proportion of farmers had adopted the new seed varieties, the rates of acceptance, and third the ultimate (ceiling) level of use, all differed between states. Broadly, compared to southern farmers, producers in the corn belt adopted the innovation earlier and more speedily and the ceiling acreage using the innovation was greater.

Differences in the date of initial acceptance (i.e. a certain minimum level of use in an area) were primarily a function of *supply* factors, that is, the availability of satisfactory hybrid seeds. This depended on the actions of the seed producers who would enter first those markets where expected profitability was highest. Expected profitability depended on a number of factors. First, the eventual market density of the area, that is, the number of acres likely to receive the innovation and the intensity of seed use. Second, the cost of marketing the product: farms in the corn belt states took sufficient seed to make it economic to have a salesman visit the farmer personally; in contrast, farms in the south were scattered and the corn acreage was much smaller. Third, the cost of innovating; the initial research produced strains of seed acceptable to farms in the corn belt area, therefore the fewer of these strains that could be adapted for use in other areas the lower the availability, further expenditure on research being necessary to develop seeds acceptable in other areas. Fourth, the expected rate of acceptance. Thus the higher the market density, the speedier the rate of acceptance, the lower the cost of innovating and marketing, the more profitable it was to enter an area, all of which induced seed suppliers to enter the corn belt area before other areas. (Similarly, for the U.K. these factors induced chemical fertilizer manufacturers to enter arable areas before grassland regions).

The other differences between areas were in the *rates of acceptance* and the ultimate *ceiling* values. Areas differed widely according to the speed with which they accepted the innovation of hybrid seed and the final proportion of acres likely to use the new seed. These differences were determined by factors on the *demand* side, the long-run supply of hybrid seed being very elastic, so that if farmers had an effective demand for the innovation, this demand could be fulfilled. These differences between areas are primarily a function of the profitability of the switch from the traditional open pollinated to the new hybrid seed. The increase in profits depends on the rise in corn yields, the price of corn (which would fall if the innovation resulted in the aggregate supply schedule of corn shifting rightwards faster than the demand schedule) and the increased cost of the hybrid seed. The rate of acceptance also depends on factors analysed previously, such as the personal characteristics of the farmer, and his financial position.

The above case study, relating the process of innovation to economic variables and drawn from an advanced country, has important implications for poor countries. On the *supply* side, once suppliers are able to produce and market non-traditional factors such as fertilizer, pesticides and hybrid seed more cheaply, then investment in agriculture becomes more profitable. The initial research on these new factors is carried out primarily in advanced countries and further research expenditures will be necessary to adapt the factors to conditions in the poorer countries, located predominantly in tropical regions. This research will have to be undertaken mainly by public bodies, as private firms are unable to obtain the research benefits, which are diffused among the firm undertaking the basic research, other firms, farmers and consumers.[1]

Similarly, it may well be unprofitable for private firms to enter poor areas, because of the small market size, the high distributive costs and the necessity to carry out extension services to educate farmers to the benefits of the innovation. At least initially, non-profit-making organizations will have to fill this gap.

1. Similarly, the separate states of the U.S.A. are unable to capture for their own farmers all the benefits of research and extension expenditures undertaken by the public agencies in the State, the new agricultural knowledge produced being extremely pervasive. See for example Latimer and Paarlberg (1965). This suggests that it is inefficient, from an economic viewpoint, to have a large number of small agricultural research agencies. This point is also made by Schultz (1964).

On the *demand* side the same economic factors discussed in the hybrid corn case study are important in influencing the demand for innovations in poor countries. Many studies emphasize the importance of the profitability of the innovations (see Schultz, 1964, pp. 164–5). Broadly, the larger the absolute yield increase compared to the cost of the innovation, the greater the incentive to adopt it. However, this statement must be qualified to the extent to which the yield increase resulting from the adoption of the new innovation is subject to greater temporal fluctuations, say because of the weather, than those experienced when using traditional inputs. Similarly, if the farm tenure arrangements are such that, whilst the farmer pays for the inputs, part of the output goes to the landlord, then the farmer, when assessing the profitability to himself of the innovation, takes account of the total increase in costs, but only that part of the increase in revenue which accrues to himself. This leads to an underestimate of the true profitability of the innovation and dampens the incentive to accept the new factor (Schultz, 1964, pp. 167–8).

4 The Role of Agriculture in Economic Growth

Aspects of Economic Growth

Economic growth has three aspects (Kuznets, 1961). The aspect normally measured is the *aggregative* which is simply the growth in gross national product. Kuznets defines economic growth as 'a sustained increase in a nation's total and *per capita* product, most often accompanied by a sustained and significant rise in population.' From an analytical viewpoint the second element in economic growth, the *structural*, is more revealing. This aspect describes the shifts that occur in the economy during the growth process, with certain industries, regions or economic groups becoming relatively more important and others less so. Thirdly, and of considerable importance for developing countries, is the *international* aspect – the process of adapting technology and know-how developed elsewhere to local conditions. Whilst this aspect is not easily quantifiable it emphasizes that economies cannot grow in an international vacuum but rather 'the changing domestic structure of a nation's economy is supplemented by a sequential pattern of economic flows between it and the rest of the world' (Kuznets, 1961, p. 57).

The aggregative, structural and international aspects of economic growth are interrelated. For example, the development of new products and processes is itself a structural change which is likely to produce a rise in incomes and may give rise to international trade flows. It is therefore impossible (and pointless) to try to allocate the contribution of agriculture under three separate heads. Rather it is necessary to consider the sector's contribution jointly in the three aspects, each element in agriculture's contribution impinging in different degree on all three aspects of economic growth.

The rediscovery of the importance of agriculture in economic growth is comparatively recent; during the 1950s most development economists looked askance at agriculture, and argued that industrialization was the dynamic element in growth. They supported this view with the generalization that the agricultural sector had redundant labour (i.e. the marginal labour productivity in agriculture was zero, or less than the institutional wage rate). Their view was typically echoed by political leaders who viewed development as synonymous with industrialization. It was generally believed that agricultural production could be expanded by eliminating a single bottleneck, though opinions differed as to whether the bottleneck in question was shortage of farm credit, lack of irrigation facilities, problems of land tenure, or inadequate communication of information (Witt, 1965).

One important reason for ignoring agriculture in the development process has been the association of agriculture with diminishing marginal returns. With a fixed land stock and constant technology, labour and capital receive decreasing returns to increased resource input. However, whilst this is nice theoretically, the assumption of constant technology is not robust enough empirically. Technical change has been as important in the agricultural sector as in the industrial sector and in consequence agriculture deserves full attention in analysis of the development process.

The focal point for empirical research into the role of agriculture was provided by Lewis who stated: 'it is not profitable to produce a growing volume of manufactures unless agricultural production is growing simultaneously. This is also why industrial and agrarian revolutions always go together, and why economies in which agriculture is stagnant do not show industrial development' (Lewis, 1954). Subsequent research generated by Lewis's article has emphasized the interrelationship of the agricultural and non-agricultural sectors in the development process, pointing towards the necessity of a balance between agricultural and industrial growth, and so correcting the widely held view that economic growth in under-developed countries must come from concentrating entirely on the industrial sector to the exclusion of agriculture.

The Special Characteristics of Agriculture in the Process of Economic Development

There are two special features of agriculture in the development process. First, agriculture is the most important industry in nearly all underdeveloped countries with typically 40–60 per cent of G.N.P. derived from agriculture and 50–80 per cent of the labour force employed in agriculture. Second, whilst contributing to economic growth the agricultural sector under-goes a secular decline relative to other sectors. This secular decline is caused by the coupling of an income elasticity of demand for food which is less than unity and declining with the fact that the rapid technical change in agriculture allows an expansion of food output with a constant or declining labour force. The decline in the agricultural sector will not proceed as rapidly or as far in those countries such as New Zealand and Denmark which have a comparative advantage in agriculture, but even in these areas less than 20 per cent of the labour force is at present in the agricultural sector (Johnston and Mellor, 1961).

The process of secular decline does not go on evenly through-out the span of development. Normally there are two elements in the process. First, the *relative* role of agriculture is reduced; it is only in the later stages of development that the far more radical element in the process, the lessening of the *absolute* role of agriculture, comes about. Normally there has been an increase in the absolute numbers employed in agriculture in the early stages of industrialization. Then the agricultural population tends to stabilize and only in the later stages does it decline absolutely.

Agriculture's Contribution to Economic Growth

Agriculture makes six contributions to economic growth:

increased food supplies, release of labour to industry, resources for industrial development, market creation, export earnings and overseas aid.

Increased food supplies

An increase in the net output of agriculture itself represents a rise in a country's G.N.P. A marked advance of food supplies is central in the chain of economic development. A rapid growth of agricultural productivity is important as it enables food supplies to be available at relatively lower prices. The non-agricultural sector then requires less of its income to purchase food, so increasing the effective demand for the output of the non-agricultural sector. This in turn increases the profitability of an expanded output in the non-agricultural sector and encourages entrepreneurs to invest there. Concurrently, expansion of the non-agricultural sector will increase the availability of job opportunities in that sector, both for the urban population and the labour released from rural areas. Furthermore, relatively declining food costs imply higher real incomes, thus reducing the pressure to increase wage earnings. This maintains or increases the profitability of investments in the non-agricultural sector. Lower food prices also reduce political discontent.

The above pattern is critical for countries in the early stages of development, which typically have a rapidly increasing population, rising demand for food and competing claims on their scarce foreign exchange supplies which therefore precludes meeting the demand for food through imports. However, the importance of an adequate food supply, from both home production and import, must not be underemphasized for advanced countries where it provides a continuous anti-inflationary force and improved nutrition.

Release of labour to industry

Industrial development requires a substantial and steady increase in manpower to facilitate expansion of output. There are three potential sources of this increased labour for the industrial sector: natural population increase, immigration and the farm population. Agriculture will be able to release labour for employment in other sectors of the economy if there is underemployment in agriculture or when improved productivity brings about a structural shift in the kind and quantity of resources used.

The release of labour stems from two sources: first, the natural increase in farm population is usually greater than that of the non-farm population, allowing a continuing outflow even with a constant farm population, thereby reducing the *relative* role of agriculture in the occupational structure of the country. Second, and normally in the later stages of development, increasing labour productivity in agriculture enables an *absolute* decrease in agricultural employment. The release of workers from agriculture represents a significant human capital contribution to the industrial sector as the bulk of the migrants will be already educated.

The major source of manpower which agriculture provides for expanding sectors occurs in the early phases of development. In the later stages of development, the absolute number of workers in agriculture may decline to the point that transfers which are a significant proportion of the current agricultural labour force represent small absolute additions to the labour force of the non-agricultural sectors. However, relatively smaller movements in more advanced countries must not be under-estimated. Out-migration from agriculture may be necessary to prevent labour shortages in other sectors.

Increased capital formation

Release of labour from the agricultural sector is one structural shift in the economy which enhances development, but economic growth cannot proceed rapidly without industrial capital – machinery, plant and transportation facilities. Agriculture makes an important contribution in permitting the formation of capital, especially in the early phases of development when agriculture produces and receives a major share of national income.

There are three ways in which the farm sector contributes to industrial capital formation. First, increased agricultural productivity benefits the non-agricultural sector through lower food prices, enlarging its real income and so providing the means for increased saving and capital accumulation in the urban sector. Second, increased output may generate higher levels of farm income, part of which may be saved. These savings may be utilized in financing the growth of the non-agricultural sectors. This contribution becomes less important in the later stages of development because as growth proceeds the relative share of a country's savings derived from agriculture becomes smaller. In generating growth it must be emphasized that it is not sufficient merely to have large agricultural savings. In addition transfer mechanisms must be available to facilitate inter-sectoral capital flows. Similarly the existence of a class of capitalist entrepreneurs sensitive to investment opportunities cannot be *assumed*. Whilst such a class did exist in, for example, Japan, it may take some time for such entrepreneurs to develop in present poor countries.

The third contribution to capital formation occurs if the government imposes a compulsory transfer of funds from agriculture for the benefit of other sectors, deriving more tax revenue from agriculture than the cost of public services to that sector, the difference being spent by the government for the benefit of the other, industrial, sector or used to finance government services. This contribution was large in the early stages of development in Japan and the Soviet Union. In the late nineteenth century the Japanese government imposed a heavy land tax which represented over 80 per cent of central government taxation: the ratio of direct taxes to income produced was 12–22 per cent in agriculture compared with 2–3 per cent in the non-agricultural sectors (Johnston, 1966). Similarly confiscation and taxation financed a considerable portion of the industrialization of the Soviet Union.

One of the major problems facing underdeveloped countries is to use agriculture to provide a basis for industrial capital accumulation without simultaneously hindering agricultural development. Some of the agricultural problems in the Soviet Union and China may be due to too rapid a diversion of agricultural resources to the non-farm sectors. The difficulties of capital formation may be mitigated for present-day under-developed countries if they are allowed access to the capital markets of the advanced countries.

Market contribution

As agriculture progresses from a subsistence sector to one producing predominantly cash crops it provides opportunities for the emergence of other sectors. There are two aspects to this 'marketization' of the economy. First, increases in agricultural productivity which result in higher *per capita* farm income allow farmers to buy more agricultural inputs and consumer goods from the industrial sector. Persistent trends stand out in present high-income countries: the spread of modern technology induces a replacement of traditional means of production which originate within the agricultural sector, for example natural fertilizer and draught animals by chemical fertilizer and tractors. This sets up a virtuous circle, the improved inputs enhancing productive efficiency in agriculture and so providing increased amounts of marketable agricultural products, over and above the farmers' own requirements, which can be exchanged for goods and services in the industrial sector.

The second element in the market contribution occurs as services such as processing, packing and distribution are developed to process and transmit the marketable agricultural produce to final consumers.

These developments occurred spontaneously in the U.S. and U.K. but inter-sectoral links may be more difficult to establish in present low-income countries. Agriculture may need to invest its surplus in non-farm capital accumulation before the industrial sector can produce final products for resale to the agricultural sector. Specifically 'agriculture may need to invest its surplus in capital accumulation for the construction of fertilizer plants before it can become a market for fertilizer as such' (Cavin *et al.*, 1963).

Whilst it may be difficult for poor countries to develop these inter-sectoral flows this market contribution is likely to be more important in the early phases of development when agriculture supplies the major proportion of the net output of the economy. The extent to which the agricultural output is traded with the other sectors has a significant influence on the width of the economic base which these other sectors may enjoy. As growth proceeds the relative share of agriculture in national product and the labour force declines and the industries in the industrial sector begin their own interaction, leading to a diminution of agriculture's market contribution.

Expansion of agricultural exports

Under-developed countries must often buy capital goods and technical know-how from present advanced countries. To be able to trade with these more advanced countries the poorer nations must develop the products in which they have a comparative advantage, typically natural resource-based industries like agriculture rather than skill-based industries. As agriculture expands its exports the revenue gained can be used both to purchase imports necessary for the development process – mainly capital goods but also some consumer goods, and pay off loans made by foreign investors. The concentration on sectors such as agriculture in which the country has a comparative advantage will not only enlarge exports, but may also contribute to economic growth via raising the nation's productive efficiency. However, an expansion in primary product supplies may lead to a reduction in their prices, thereby turning the terms of trade against the primary producers.

Assisting developing nations

The final contribution to growth is one made by U.S. agriculture. Now that the agricultural sector in the U.S. generates only a minor proportion of G.N.P. its contribution to domestic economic growth is less than in the past. It is in aid to developing nations that it may still make a major contribution. There are two elements here, technical assistance and direct food shipments. Whilst U.S. agriculture has accumulated a tremendous stock of technological and managerial know-how the transfer of this knowledge involves the process of adapting it to local conditions. The bulk of the poor countries are located in tropical regions whereas the U.S. is located in the temperate zone. This implies that the agronomist must develop crop varieties which are suitable to these tropical regions.

Second, American agriculture has 'its most direct and dramatic opportunity for promoting world economic growth through programmes that supply surplus food to under-developed countries' (Cavin *et al.*, 1963). Whilst the exact role of food aid has yet to be evaluated food shipments can aid development by, for example, improving the health of the labour force, acting as a damper on inflation, and raising real incomes.

The elements of the specific contribution of agriculture have now been described. The last contribution, direct food ship-ments from the U.S. to developing countries, gives a clue to what the crucial development problem is for these countries, namely *increasing food production* and it is to this problem of agricultural development that we now turn.

Agricultural Development

The problem of population growth

Perhaps the most important factor limiting efforts to raise *per capita* real incomes in under-developed countries is their rapid growth of population. Typically the total population is expanding around 2–3 per cent per annum with the non-agricul-tural population expanding somewhat faster than the agri-cultural population. The prospect of continued growth of the agricultural population and labour force in developing coun-tries has important implications for agricultural development planning, especially in densely populated countries where opportunities for expanding the land area under cultivation are limited. This can be demonstrated by a simple example (based on Christensen, 1966). The assumptions are that 70 per cent of the total population of a developing country is in agriculture and that between 1965 and A.D. 2000 the total population increases 2·5 per cent a year, and the non-agricul-tural population increases 4 per cent a year (Table 10). In this case the agricultural population increases 1·5 per cent a year. The country would make the transition from 70 per cent to

50 per cent of total population in agriculture by the year 2000. The total, non-agricultural and agricultural populations would increase (approximately) 140,300 and 70 per cent respectively. In fact population growth rates in many of the poor countries are likely to increase in excess of the assumed 2·5 per cent a year – implying that the agricultural population of some countries may *double* before it begins to decrease.

The rapid population increase implies that low-income countries will require far larger increases in agricultural production than those achieved in nearly all the developed countries during the early stages of their development. In the example cited total agricultural supply would need to increase by 3·1 per cent a year to meet demands stemming from population growth and slowly rising *per capita* incomes. If the country does not have a spare margin of land available for cultivation then production per unit of land will have to increase by the same amount as total production (3·1 per cent or virtually triple by the year 2000 in the example, or more if the population is increasing at a greater annual rate than 2·5 per cent).

Before discussing the stock of methods by which under-developed countries can achieve greater production, it is necessary to mention a further problem brought on by rapid population growth. Given many under-developed countries (for example India, Pakistan, Turkey, Philippines, Egypt) have a constant land stock which is already being cultivated, how will the sizes of farms need to change as the agricultural labour force increases? Should resources in agriculture be combined as family size units, or should large farms, employing say ten or more workers be established? The under-developed countries cannot look for guidance at the historical experience of presently advanced countries as the circumstances are different. The U.S., Canada, Australia and New Zealand all experienced rapid population growth but had large areas of virgin land which they brought into cultivation as the agricultural population increased. In Western Europe and Japan the total population growth of around 1 per cent per annum was significantly slower than that being experienced by present poor

Table 10
Projected Growth Rates for Population and Agricultural
Production in a Typical Developing Country, 1965 to 2000

Item	Annual growth rate	Year 1965	2000	Percentage increase
Population:	per cent	million	million	per cent
Total	2·5	100	237	137
Non-agricultural	4·0	30	119	296
Agricultural	1·5	70	118	68
		per cent	per cent	
Agricultural production:				
Total[1]	3·1	100	291	191
Per hectare	3·1	100	291	191
Per farm worker	1·6	100	173	73

1. Total agricultural production projected to meet increase in economic demand, assuming annual income growth of 1 per cent per person and income elasticity of demand for farm products of 0·6, in addition to population growth.

countries and the European and Japanese agricultural populations remained approximately stationary in the early stages of development.

The economic answer to the question of whether farm size should be reduced or the number of workers per farm should be increased hinges on the effect of structural change on crop yields – a problem of economies or diseconomies of size. Empirical evidence on economies of size in agriculture is very sketchy but, for example, Japan and Taiwan have achieved high productivity per land unit with very small farms. Similarly studies of Japan, Iran and India indicate that average crop yields are higher on small than on large farms (Brown, 1965), but further research is necessary before conclusions can be drawn for agricultural development strategy.

Methods to increase food production
The critical factor in improving food production lies in increasing grain yields. Grains account for 71 per cent of the

world's harvested crop area; they provide 53 per cent of man's supply of food energy when consumed directly and a large part of the remainder when consumed indirectly in the form of meat, milk and eggs (Brown, 1965, p. 10). We are not presenting here either an exhaustive list of yield-increasing practices nor a framework of agricultural development strategy, but rather emphasizing some of the problems which occur in agricultural development.[1] Initially it is necessary to develop the *agricultural pre-conditions* (or phase I). That is, the ability of the existing labour-intensive agriculture to absorb innovations which increase output per unit of input must be increased. This can be achieved via both economic and institutional policy instruments. On the economic side it may be necessary to improve agricultural product prices, but simultaneously policy makers will possibly have to change land tenure arrangements, improve credit facilities so that farmers can acquire new inputs and improve marketing arrangements to ensure that the increased agricultural output reaches non-farm consumers.

In the early stages of agricultural development it will probably be necessary to minimize the reliance on purchased inputs. This is phase II of the Johnston–Mellor framework: expanding agricultural production by labour-intensive, capital-saving techniques, relying heavily on technical innovations. It is necessary to emphasize innovations which do not require large increases in the use of purchased inputs, such as high-yielding seed varieties, improved crop rotation or multiple cropping because in the early stages of development the money income of the agricultural sector will be small unless it has large export sales. However, it is necessary to have some bought-in inputs, especially fertilizer. Phase II of agricultural development is characterized by a high degree of *complementarity* between conventional inputs and 'non-conventional' inputs. The best example of this complementarity is between the conventional fertilizer input and the non-conventional improved seed varieties. There are two aspects here: on the one hand traditional seed varieties in under-developed countries are likely to be

1. This sketch of the problems follows closely the model of agricultural development of Johnston and Mellor (1961).

unresponsive to increase in fertilizer application. On the other hand some improved, high-yielding seeds only function properly with fertilizers; in Japan, for example, the combination of new rice strains and increased fertilizer input was primarily responsible for agricultural development.[1]

In the later stages of development agricultural production can be expanded by more capital-intensive methods (phase III) such as increased mechanization and large-scale drainage and irrigation projects. However, the central problem for present low income countries remains how to expand agricultural production without using capital required for the industrial sectors; thus the capital available for bought-in inputs is likely to remain small, making it all the more necessary to try to achieve the correct marginal balance among inputs such as fertilizer, seed and irrigation projects which do require funds and are complementary in the process of development.

1. Japanese fertilizer experience gives a clue to a further important development factor, where, in addition to an increased demand for fertilizer, innovations in the fertilizer industry shifted the supply schedule out, causing a decline in the relative price and induced an increased application of fertilizer. Thus, complementarity also exists between innovations in the fertilizer industry and innovations in agriculture.

5 The Structure of Agricultural Markets

Students of agricultural marketing have devoted attention to three main subjects. First, the determination of patterns of consumer demand, and estimates of the price and income elasticities of demand. Second, examination of the efficiency of the price system in giving expression to the preferences of consumers and guidance to the allocation of resources. Third, marketing is examined more narrowly to determine the operational efficiency of the agricultural marketing chain, that is, the cost incurred in getting output from farmer to consumer. An agricultural product is produced in a given place at a given time: the aim is to minimize both the cost of production and the cost of the further processes necessary to get the product to the consumer, for example, assembling, processing, storage, transport and distribution.

In this and the following chapter we are broadly concerned with the price and cost efficiency aspects of marketing and not with analysis of the demand for farm products.[1] This chapter presents the outline of market structure analysis, which facilitates an assessment of the efficiency of the industries comprising the agricultural marketing chain. The following chapter analyses the more important institutional arrangements which occur in the agricultural marketing chain such as vertical integration, contract farming, producer co-operatives and marketing boards, which are, partly at least, designed to raise farm incomes through intervention in the market.

A major feature of agricultural marketing is the declining share which farmers receive of the final retail food price. In the United States farmers received 51 per cent of the retail cost of

1. For analysis of the demand for farm products see Shepherd (1962), 4th edn, chs. 3–8 and Waugh (1964).

food in 1947; by 1965 they received only 39 per cent. It is sometimes alleged that this apparent worsening of the farmers' position is due to exploitation by distributors. Whilst this statement may be partly true in the case of certain commodities it is generally based on a misreading of both the causes of relatively low agricultural incomes and the determinants of the final retail price. The reasons that agricultural incomes are frequently low compared with those in other industries are analysed in chapter 7 and will not detain us here. However, it is not, of course, legitimate to present the 'agricultural income problem' in terms of the proportion of the retail food expenditure accruing to the agricultural sector, as it is perfectly feasible to envisage a future situation where farmers only receive, say, 10 per cent of the final retail price yet have higher incomes than equivalent industrial workers. The fundamental reason for the declining farmers' share is that the income elasticity of demand for food services (for example restaurant meals, convenience and frozen foods) is substantially higher than that for the food itself; thus as income rises the farmers' share of total consumer expenditure on food declines. Increased costs of inputs used by the processing and distribution sectors in the marketing chain and higher taxation levels are also responsible for the rise in final prices, although they have been partially offset by higher productivity.

Some of the institutional methods by which farmers have attempted to raise their incomes and thereby offset their declining shares in final retail price are analysed in the next chapter, but first we turn to market structure analysis, which provides models which may be used to assess the performance of the agricultural marketing chain.

The Structure–Conduct–Performance Relationship

The agricultural sector is intimately linked with other industries and is affected by the efficiency of these industries. Agriculture has links with industries which process and distribute the basic agricultural output, for example meat packing and milk distribution. Similarly, food retailers are linked backwards in the marketing chain to food manufacturers, and in some cases, for example broilers, to agriculture itself. It is therefore of fundamental importance to provide some guidelines which assist an evaluation of the efficiency of these industries, each link in the agricultural marketing chain, including the final consumer, being affected by the performance of the other elements of the chain.

Such an analytical framework is provided by market structure analysis.[1] In this section we trace the development of market structure analysis and indicate its theoretical basis. Reference will be made to empirical analyses of market structure in the industries involved in the agricultural marketing chain, from input suppliers to retail outlets. This will provide examples of the hypotheses generated by the underlying theoretical model and of tests made to assess the validity of these hypotheses. The aim of market structure analysis is two-fold. First, to determine whether a relationship exists between the structure of an industry, the behaviour of the firms which comprise that industry and the overall economic performance of the industry. Second, to compare the actual structure, conduct and performance dimensions with certain dimensions generally considered desirable.

The development of the analytical framework started from the concept of perfect competition. It is only under a perfectly competitive price system that the marginal rules ensuring optimum resource allocation are fulfilled.[2] Perfect competition was therefore used as a standard against which to evaluate actual industry structures. However, the extension of the theory of the firm in the 1930s to incorporate the theories of Robinson and Chamberlain (1933) emphasized that perfect competition had never existed and was an unreal standard for comparative

1. For more detailed accounts of market structure research in agricultural economics see Clodius and Mueller (1961) and Moore and Walsh (1966). The latter reference provides a comprehensive analysis of the market structure of fourteen agricultural industries and bravely presents a normative evaluation of these sectors.

2. For full details of these marginal rules and proof of their fulfilment under perfectly competitive conditions see Baumol (1962), ch. 13.

purposes in that it could never be achieved. Also it was questioned whether perfect competition provided a normative ideal, for whilst it led to optimum resource allocation, it did so only with regard to a particular income distribution which itself might not be ideal, a different income distribution almost certainly resulting in a different optimal resource allocation. These defects of the perfectly competitive standard were accentuated by the fact that it is essentially a static concept, not catering for the dynamic aspects of technical progressiveness. Thus Schumpeter (1942) suggested that monopoly may be more conducive to technological development and economic growth than competition.[1]

The overthrow of the norm of perfect competition led to the development of the concept of *workable competition* which was concerned to set forth the most desirable form of competition, given certain inherent degrees of imperfection (Clarke, 1940); that is, it attempted to establish practically attainable conditions, the workability criteria, for the particular sector(s). The dimensions of workable competition are typically placed in the three broad categories of market structure, firm conduct and industry performance. The theoretical model is both deterministic and sequential, the direction of causation running from structure through firm behaviour to the performance of the industry. However, whether performance is satisfactory cannot be inferred from fulfilment of requirements for structure and conduct, which rather is necessary but not sufficient for

1. Further defects in the competitive norm are as follows. First, overall resource allocation may be worse if some industries are monopolies and others perfectly competitive than if all industries are monopolies, i.e. some competition may be worse than none. Second, say there are five pre-requisites for perfect competition, all equally essential, but one is lacking. Now it no longer follows that we are better off because of the presence of the remaining four conditions, some or all of which may be positively detrimental. Suppose, for example, that the pre-requisite of perfect factor mobility (i.e. freedom of entry and exit) is missing, but the other requirements are met. Now let the demand for the industry's product decline. Competition will now be deemed 'too strong' and the industry 'sick'. These are inter- and intra-industry aspects of the familiar problem of 'second-best'.

the attainment of satisfactory performance.[1] The market structure analysis model is concerned ultimately with the (normative) aspect of industry performance, and suggests hypotheses regarding the linkage between the three elements market structure, firm conduct and industry performance. Whilst the linkage between these components is far from substantiated in all cases, the structure–conduct–performance model provides a useful framework for analysing an individual industry. In this section no attempt is made to develop an overall model. Instead we examine the variables which can be included under the broad categories of structure, conduct and performance and give examples of the links between these categories.

Market Structure

The elements of market structure consist of those characteristics of the organization of a market which seem to influence strategically the nature of competition and pricing within the market. Here we discuss three important dimensions of market structure: concentration among sellers, conditions of entry and vertical integration.

Degree of seller concentration

The degree of seller concentration is described by the number and size distribution of sellers in the market. Whilst economic theory offers clues regarding the likely absolute size of firms, as functions of technology and factor costs, it offers no guidelines, except in the limiting cases of perfect competition and monopoly, about the likely size distribution of firms. Given the size of the market, absolute plant and firm size will vary according to technology and input prices; alternatively, given technology, the number of plants will vary with market size. Thus from price theory we may predict the probable effect of input costs and market size on the absolute size and number of firms, but this does not permit predictions about relative size.

Measures of concentration were developed to fill this gap.

1. For a discussion and appraisal of workable competition see Sosnick (1958).

The simplest measure of the degree of concentration is the percentage share of sales (or employment, assets or other variables) accounted for by the largest n firms, where n is typically 4, 8 and 20.[1] A knowledge of the extent of concentration is important in providing predictions regarding the behaviour of the firms in the industry, affecting for example price, output and technical progressiveness. The strategic position of grocery retailing outlets in the agricultural marketing chain has led to a number of studies into the degree of concentration in that industry and the effect of this concentration on the behaviour of the firms in their dealings with farmers, food manufacturers, processors and consumers.[2] Typically the over-all degree of concentration in the industry is low; in the U.S.A. in 1958 the top twenty grocery chains controlled only an average of 1·8 per cent of national sales each, and in the U.K. in 1966 organizations with over 100 outlets controlled only 7·9 per cent of the total number of outlets. However, to assess the impact of concentration on firm conduct, it is necessary to define the relevant market. For example, retailers may buy in regional or national markets, but the relevant selling market is far smaller, normally the city level, or a smaller city sub-market. Therefore if we wish our economic model to provide us with realistic hypotheses regarding firms' selling policies it is totally irrelevant that the overall national degree of concentration is low. Instead the degree of concentration at the local level must be calculated, and this is typically far higher than that prevailing at national level. We discuss the impact of this structure variable on firm conduct below.

Conditions of entry into an industry

This dimension refers to the relative ease or difficulty with which new sellers may enter the market, and is determined by the advantages which established sellers have over potential

1. Alternatively, the degree of concentration may be measured by the Lorenz curve/Gini coefficient which measures the degree of inequality in firm size over the whole industry, see for example Hart and Prais (1956).

2. See for example, for the U.S.A., Mueller and Garoain (1961) and for the U.K., Metcalf (1968).

entrants. This characteristic therefore has a fundamental bearing on firm conduct in that it determines the amount by which existing firms can raise price above cost without inducing new entrants, that is, it sets the 'entry forestalling price'. There are three main types of entry barrier.

Scale economies. This type of entry barrier arises where firms do not achieve lowest unit production costs until they attain an output which is a relatively large proportion of the total industry output. Take for example the case of ammonia for nitrogenous fertilizers in the U.K.

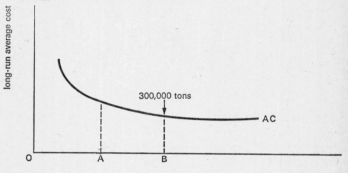

Figure 9 Scale economy entry barriers in the production of nitrogenous fertilizer

The minimum technically optimum plant scale is one with an output of 300,000 tons per annum, which comprises around one sixth of the ammonia output required for nitrogenous fertilizer. Thus a potential new entrant into this industry faces a dilemma. There are two alternatives: the firm can build a plant of size OB thereby achieving the prevailing scale economies, but to sell this output the firm would have to penetrate the market of existing firms, probably by price cutting which would almost certainly provoke retaliation. Alternatively, the firm could build a plant with a smaller output OA which has higher unit costs. The extent of the penalty imposed on the firm in this latter case depends on the steepness of the average cost curve to the left of output OB.

Absolute cost barriers. This entry barrier includes anything that raises the average production cost of a new firm above that of existing firms of *all* output levels. It may be caused by existing firms having detailed knowledge ('know-how') concerning production techniques, or through patents. Alternatively, firms may have gained control, possibly through vertical integration, of a limited supply of a significant input; they are therefore able to raise the costs of their competitors by charging them a relatively high price for this input. This entry barrier tends to be relatively unimportant in the industries ancillary to agriculture.

Product differentiation.[1] In the same way that absolute cost barriers raise the production costs of new entrants, product differentiation erects an entry barrier in that it raises selling costs at all levels of output. Suppose, for example, that a new food retail outlet sets up in competition with existing outlets. It is unlikely to encounter entry barriers of the scale economy or absolute cost type, but its selling costs will almost certainly be higher initially than those of its competitors, as it will have to mount a campaign to differentiate its product in the eyes of the consumer, through, for example, better parking facilities, a better deal on special offers, or home deliveries. Similarly, a new entrant into fertilizer or tractor manufacturing would have to gain acceptance of its product by farmers, for example via advertising in the technical journals or visits to the farm by the firm's salesmen. In contrast, a new entrant into farming will face no such entry barrier, the buyers being indifferent to the origin of the product.

Vertical integration[2]

The extent of vertical integration, loosely defined as control

1. This is frequently presented as a characteristic of market structure in its own right, but here it is placed as a subdivision of the entry barrier characteristic.

2. Vertical integration as a dimension of market structure is only considered briefly here. The vertically integrated relationships among agriculture and related industries are analysed in chapter 6.

over more than one stage of production by a single decision-making unit, is a further important structural dimension. In both the U.K. and the U.S.A. there has been a shift in the balance of power between food retailers and their suppliers in favour of the former. This is not the result of increasing market concentration in retailing but is rather directly attributable to the increasing ease with which grocery retailers can integrate into grocery manufacturing and develop their own brands; this private label selling by chains can successfully undermine the differentiated product of the food manufacturer. In those sectors where retail chains have integrated backwards, for example baking, dairying and meat packing, the food manufacturers' profits have fallen. Similarly, the threat of vertical integration by the chains into other food retailing sectors has induced food manufacturers to price more competitively. The potential threat of forward vertical integration by manufacturers into retailing is far more remote, firstly because they would need large capital investment to obtain sufficient outlets for a significant proportion of their output, and secondly, because they would jeopardize existing retail outlets in that they would be competing at retail level with their own customers.

This brief discussion shows that the characteristics of market structure may have a significant influence on the behaviour of the firms comprising the industry, and it is to this conduct component of market structure analysis that we now turn.

Firm Conduct

This may be defined as 'patterns of behaviour which enterprises follow in adapting or adjusting to the markets in which they sell or buy.' Conduct therefore refers to the actions, dealings or tactics of enterprises in their own markets or towards their rivals in that market, including policies towards setting prices and quality or aimed at coercing rivals.

We know from the theory of the firm that each major industry type from perfect competition to monopoly provides different scope for firms in choosing their behaviour patterns. Under perfect competition the individual firm, once the decision of what to produce has been taken, has very little freedom of choice: the market sets the price, there is nothing to be gained by individual advertising, the firm also has no choice regarding efficiency, it must keep its costs as low as possible or go out of business.[1] By contrast, a monopoly has a number of possible objective functions: it may, for example, attempt to maximize sales, prestige or profits.

The most complex patterns of firm behaviour stem from oligopolistic market structures, where firms recognize their mutual interdependence.[2] The retail grocery market, on the selling side, typically has an oligopolistic market structure, in that individual retail sub-markets are spatially diffuse and tend to be highly concentrated; also, the few sellers are closely linked in their demand functions (that is, the cross elasticities of demand for the products of individual outlets are high). However, given that firms do not all buy in the same wholesale market, thereby precluding agreement on margins, the only way to achieve and maintain agreement on prices is via price leadership. In fact little evidence exists to substantiate the existence of price leadership, rather, studies suggest widespread dispersion of prices rather than price leadership (Metcalf and Greenhalgh, 1968). This lack of oligopoly agreement is probably due to the fact that whilst sub-markets are highly concentrated the barriers to entry into retailing are relatively low. We must be careful therefore to formulate our predictions of firm

1. This statement should be qualified. If all firms in the industry are equally *inefficient* then any one firm will not have to attain its lowest *absolute* unit costs to remain in the industry, but rather must attain costs levels similar to the other firms.

2. This mutual interdependence is greatest with a duopoly (two firms) structure and becomes less pronounced the greater the number of firms. Behaviour of firms under an oligopolistic market structure is frequently likened to a game of chess or poker. For example, one strategy which firms may follow is to attempt to maximize the damage to the opponent, whilst simultaneously minimizing the damage he can do to you. There are a number of other possible strategies (patterns of conduct) and these are incorporated into the body of knowledge known as the theory of games.

conduct only after allowing for all features of market structure rather than just relying on one element, in this case the degree of concentration, to give prediction.

The normative aspect of market structure analysis attempts to determine whether the resulting firm conduct is 'reasonable'. The difficulty here is to achieve a consensus on what constitutes satisfactory conduct but there is general consensus that: firms should strive in rivalry, pursuing their independent judgement and responding without collusion to considerations of profit and loss; there should be no unfair, exclusionary, predatory or coercive tactics; sales promotion policy should not be misleading.[1]

Industry Performance

Market structure analysis is ultimately concerned with how well industries perform, which refers to the economic results which flow from the industry as an aggregate of firms. Broadly, we wish to know (a) how well industries perform,[2] (b) what explains the good and bad features of their performance, and (c) how performance can be improved, for example, through

1. These behaviour norms refer to the desired conduct of firms inside the country. In contrast it is frequently considered permissible or even desirable that our firms engaging in international trade collude with each other.

2. It is necessary here to disentangle the positive and normative elements of performance. The choice of the dimensions comprising performance and an evaluation of the workability of an industry with respect to these dimensions is normative, each commentator being able to choose his own norms and make his own assessment of whether the firms in the industry are workably competitive. This has inevitably led to conflicts over both what constitute desirable norms and whether the economic results flowing from the industry with respect to these norms are reasonable. In contrast the actual testing of hypotheses is positive. Take the example of sales promotion expenditure; the inclusion of this as a relevant performance dimension is a normative decision on the part of the researchers; the testing of the hypothesis, say, that firms in highly concentrated industries have a higher ratio of sales promotion expenditure to total revenue is positive; the final evaluation of the reasonableness of the firms performance in this dimension is normative.

public policy such as anti-trust legislation. Let us look briefly at three important aspects of performance.

Technical progressiveness

This must be judged in relation to the possibilities to innovate, science-based industries having greater potential to innovate than the more traditional craft-based industries.[1] We can, however, isolate certain undesirable performance elements such as supression of inventions and inadequate diffusion of innovations. Research suggests that a competitive market structure makes for a widespread diffusion of innovations. For agriculture the research into and development of new innovations is done mainly by public bodies or input suppliers, no one firm being large enough to finance its own research. Once a new innovation is adopted by a few farmers the competitive market structure makes for a fairly speedy and widespread diffusion of the innovation, which benefits society in the form of lower food prices.[2] The food retailing industry too has been highly progressive, catering for the increased demand for more highly processed, packaged foodstuffs and changing its organization so that the bulk of sales are now through self-service outlets.

Economic efficiency

Efficiency is primarily concerned with resource allocation, both between industries and inside individual industries. Market structure analysis uses the notion of normal profits as an indicator of proper resource allocation.[3] Short-run profits will diverge from long-run normal profits when demand is under-

1. This point is frequently overlooked when the rate of technical progressiveness is related to the average size of the firm and it is found industries consisting of large firms are progressive. They may be progressive not because of large size *per se* but because they tend to be science-based.

2. But does not necessarily benefit the agricultural sector itself; this high rate of technical progressiveness is a major cause of the agricultural income problem analysed in chapter 7.

3. We may view normal profits as the opportunity cost of equity capital, that is, the minimum normal profit rate based on what the investment funds could earn elsewhere.

or over-estimated, thus signalling the need for resource re-allocation. Research suggests a definite relationship between market structure and profit rates, more highly concentrated industries with high entry barriers attaining excess profits (Bain, 1951). One of the main causes of low agricultural incomes and low returns received by small shopkeepers is that the signal of relatively low profits has not been acted upon, resources have not flowed out of the industries quickly enough.[1]

If we wished to assess the economic efficiency of the firms in an industry, where economic efficiency is measured by how closely the firms in the industry approximate the lowest attainable costs for the outputs they produce and distribute, we would consider the following three aspects of economic efficiency.

First, is the output of the industry being produced by plants and firms which exhaust all the available economies of scale of production and distribution? The explanation of the continuance of large numbers of inefficient, small-capacity plants in certain industries may be partly explained by the structural characteristic of product differentiation. In the grocery sector, for example, it has been claimed that individual stores tend to have a small faithful clientele who are prepared to pay more than they would at other stores for a similar basket of goods.

For both plants and firms the importance of diseconomies of small scale depends, with reference to Figure 9, on the steepness of the rise in the AC curve to the left of output OB. That is, for any product, if unit costs rise sharply for a plant which is smaller than the minimum optimum size OB then obviously it is far more important that the output of that product is supplied by plants which do attain economies of scale than if the AC curve (unit costs) only rises very gently to the left of OB. That is, in this latter case the rise in unit costs in the plants having

1. This poses a fundamental point. It may be that the labour resources in agriculture which are receiving low returns stay in the industry because of non-pecuniary factors. In exactly the same way society may decide it does not want the upheavals which accompany rapid technical change. In this brief excursion into market structure analysis all we are doing is suggesting certain economic dimensions, and not concerning ourselves with such trade-off problems.

diseconomies of small scale is not so serious. Evidence suggests that, for firms in a number of industries, the AC curve generally rises gently to the left of output OB (Caves, 1968).

Thus the rise in a firm's unit costs caused by having plants of a scale smaller than the optimum may well be far smaller than the rise in unit costs due to other causes such as inadequate vertical integration and poor stock control. In effect then there are two sets of factors which cause costs to rise above the minimum. First, diseconomies of (either too large or too small) scale; that is, despite using the 'best' production technique for the *given* level of output, unit costs are higher, because output is either too small or too large, than for an alternative level of output. Second, taking the horizontal scale of production as *given*, other factors such as internal inefficiency and inadequate vertical integration might cause unit costs to rise above the minimum for that particular output level.[1]

Therefore the second aspect of economic efficiency to be considered is whether the firms in the industry have the correct degree of vertical integration. For example, are the technically complementary productive processes undertaken in a single plant? The third aspect is whether the aggregate capacity in the industry is correct, or whether excess or insufficient capacity exists.

The problems of measuring the performance of an industry with respect to these components of economic efficiency are very real. For example, when considering economies of scale judgements must be made about the time it takes for small firms to grow up, the competence of management and the extent to which production economies gained by concentrating production in fewer plants would be offset by increased transport and distribution costs.

Similarly, when assessing the correctness or otherwise of the aggregate capacity of an industry the following would have to be taken into account: whether or not the firm(s) had deliberately expanded ahead of demand; the extent of the variability of demand, perhaps due to seasonal factors; and whether or

1. Unit costs change, then, in the first instance through *moving along* the AC curve, and in the second through a *shift* in the curve itself.

not it is cheaper to obtain a plant's minimum AC or to under-utilize a larger plant.

These factors make it virtually impossible to make a meaningful test of a firm's *absolute* efficiency (i.e. actual costs compared with the minimum possible costs). Rather it is necessary to examine a firm's efficiency relative to that of other firms and concentrate on detecting certain departures from minimum costs which are quite apparent.

Sales promotion expenditure

A third factor which has frequently been considered when assessing the performance of firms and industries is sales promotion expenditure. Frequently distinctions have been drawn between informative and persuasive advertising, the former being in some sense more acceptable than the latter. However, such distinctions should not be carried too far as informative advertising is to some extent persuasive and vice versa. Satisfactory or unsatisfactory performance has typically been judged in terms of the relationship between advertising expenditure and total revenue, or by a comparison of the amount spent on research compared with expenditure on advertising. It is perhaps more difficult to lay down criteria for 'good' and 'bad' performance with respect to advertising than with the other performance dimensions considered. For example, heavy advertising expenditure *may* shift the demand curve for each firm to the right. If the firms in the industry face a decreasing cost schedule then this lowers unit costs; and these lower costs may then be passed on to the consumer in the form of lower prices. However, this is not the place for an examination of the case for and against advertising. Suffice it to say that the extent and amount of advertising might be relevant when attempting to assess the performance of a particular industry.

We now leave market structure analysis which provides a scaffolding on which to build in assessing the performance of the agricultural industry itself and the industries ancillary to agriculture. The next chapter considers a number of the institutional arrangements by which farmers have attempted to raise their incomes.

6 Contract Farming and Marketing Boards

Contract Farming and Vertical Integration

In the post-war period the traditional links among the institutions comprising the agricultural marketing chain have, in a number of cases, been fundamentally altered through more widespread use of vertical integration and contracts. It is necessary to distinguish between vertical integration and contractual arrangements although they are sometimes referred to interchangeably. In this chapter we analyse contractual arrangements and vertical integration reaching forward from farmers. We are not concerned with integration between food processors and retailers. *Vertical integration* may be defined as 'ownership or control by one company of enterprises in different stages of production or distribution, where each stage yields a saleable commodity.'[1] The key word in this definition is control, by which is meant the power to subjugate the profits of a firm at one stage of production to that of a firm at another stage. By adopting this definition contracting becomes a separate practice from vertical integration, rather than one possible vertically integrated structure, for the parties to contractual arrangements continue to make their decisions with a view to maximizing their own objective function (normally profits) rather than the profits of some other larger organization as is the case with full vertical integration.

We may therefore define *contracting* as 'a temporary undertaking by one independent company to produce for or buy from another independent company.' Firms enter a contract because they feel that it gives greater absolute benefits than alternative strategies, for example farmers may feel that the

1. This definition and that of contracting is taken from Trifon (1959).

benefits they receive from selling poultry or pigs through contractual arrangements are greater than those attained via the open market. The 'benefits' include non-pecuniary factors as well as purely monetary returns. For example, the farmer may receive higher absolute average income over a period by selling in the open market, but he may nevertheless prefer contracting and a somewhat lower income as he knows the price in advance and this price fluctuates much less severely through time than the free market price. Thus whilst there may be bargaining between the farmer and the other party to the contract the farmer is less concerned about his relative position compared to the other party than with the return he received through contracting (or vertical integration) compared with the return from the alternative course of action.

Let us turn now to the advantages of having institutional links with adjacent industries rather than relying on the price mechanism for coordination of production and marketing activities. We then indicate some of the reasons why these links have predominantly taken the form of contractual agreements rather than full vertical integration. The farmer may prefer to establish these institutional links for a number of reasons; first, because of the income instability which results from the framework of the traditional marketing system, although this is partly mitigated by guaranteed price schemes. This inherent instability of prices and incomes may cause difficulties in meeting interest repayments on capital or may be disliked merely because of the uncertainty. The farmer is therefore happy to shift the risk for the bearing of this price and income uncertainty on to some other party, preferring the guarantee of a specified price per unit of the commodity. Second, these institutional arrangements have given farmers access to more sources of capital than are provided through the banking system. Thus input suppliers and food manufacturers, anxious that the farmer achieves technical efficiency and uses their product, are prepared to loan him the necessary funds, often at favourable interest rates. Third, farmers are frequently conscious that they lack the expertise necessary to cope with modern technology and are prepared to enter into these arrangements to obtain full technical advice both on production methods as well as on, for example, modern cost accounting techniques. The assurance of a ready market for their produce is a further reason from the viewpoint of the farmers.

A major reason why food manufacturers have developed links backward with agriculture has been to attain a continuous flow of agricultural output, which is perishable or costly to store. This is especially important for those manufacturers, for example broiler processors, who have high fixed costs and who therefore desire to keep their productive capacity as fully utilized as possible. Similarly, fruit and vegetable canners have developed backward links with agriculture because of the peculiar biological nature of agricultural output. As there is a significant gestation period in agricultural production the short run elasticity of supply is often less than one; this implies that competition between canners for available supplies will not lead to an increase in output, but rather to a price rise, and they have therefore attempted to guarantee their share of the sales by establishing links with growers at planting. Backward links also enable food manufacturers to secure greater control over the quality of the product, which is especially important where advertising concentrates on quality differentials rather than price.

Higher *per capita* incomes and a larger proportion of women working have led to a much increased demand for convenience foods such as pre-packed bacon and poultry and frozen vegetables. The demand specifications of texture, taste, colour, proportion of lean to fat meat, for example, are relatively complex, and it is difficult to reflect these specifications back to the farmer purely in terms of the price of the product. Therefore to ensure uniformity of the product in sufficient volume backward links have been established among retailers, processors and farmers.

Farmers have also been affected by forward integration. A prime mover in establishing links between input suppliers and agriculture has been the feed producing industry where the desire to increase the sales of feed led to the innovations of dry feed lots and broiler factories. Forward links with agriculture were established for the now familiar reasons of lack of detailed knowledge of the new methods by farmers, lethargy of farmers in adjusting to these new capital-intensive techniques, and the fact that the agricultural sector lacked the capital funds to implement the innovations. The feed firms therefore advanced credit for the provision of necessary buildings and machinery, arranged supply of the chicks or feeder cattle, advanced the feed, provided the necessary veterinary services and supervised the marketing of the final product.

Thus there are a number of technical and economic reasons why all sectors in the agricultural marketing chain, input suppliers, farmers, manufacturers and retailers, may prefer to establish links with adjacent sectors rather than depend solely on the open market to coordinate their actions. The incidence of these institutional arrangements appears strongest in those sectors of agricultural production where capital requirements are substantial and where the growing to selling period is short as in broilers and fruit and vegetable production. These links have been predominantly of a contractual nature, rather than full vertical integration. From the farmers' viewpoint the lack of complete vertical integration may be explained relatively easily. Under most vertically integrated relationships the integrator (initiator) would be the sector other than agriculture and it would therefore be the farmer's decisions that were controlled and his profits subjugated; this would leave him the status of a hired hand and typically farmers prefer to retain some decision-making functions for themselves. Among the reasons why the other sectors too have preferred contractual arrangements are the following: first, a number of farms are mixed, that is, grow products other than those which are the subject of the contract; contracting therefore avoids the additional responsibilities of finding a market for these products. Second, the capital requirements of entering agriculture, in terms of the cost of land, buildings and machinery, would be substantial; third, linked with the second reason, there is considerable advantage to be obtained by letting the tenant or landlord bear the cost of the land. The integrator tends to obtain the land and equipment relatively cheaply, in that the cost of the vacant possession in most countries is greater than the value of rent the farmer pays. Fourth, the urge to integrate may only be temporary, the integrator not wishing to enter long-run commitments.

These contractual arrangements bring problems to the farmer as well as benefits in that they tend to speed up existing trends and therefore accentuate the problems of agricultural adjustment. For example, the adoption of new technology is hastened, accentuating the pressure on supplies; this is especially likely if contracts are accompanied by significant credit extension, which facilitates the adoption of the most technically efficient production methods. The resulting increases in supply lead to downward pressure on prices and possibly lower incomes for non-contracting farmers. These arrangements also lead to fundamental changes in the farm structure. They encourage both fewer, larger holdings and increased specialization, so that the size of individual enterprises can be enlarged to fully achieve the prevailing scale economies. This trend to specialization and more rapid technical change is likely to lead to both a reduction in the numbers employed in agriculture, and a decline in the managerial role of those farmers remaining. The farmer may well lack the specialized skills and technical know-how required by the contractor, who will provide these himself, leaving the farmer with caretaker functions. This decline in the managerial role will go furthest where the producer is completely specialized, for example citrus fruits, rather than if the farmer contracts only one of a number of crops or livestock products.

The fundamental changes wrought in the agricultural marketing chain by the substitution of these forward and backward links with agriculture for the traditional reliance on the price mechanism have induced a number of reactions in agriculture itself, mainly in an attempt to retain the decision making in the hands of the farmer or his representative rather than with an input supplier or food manufacturer. What, then, are the options open to the farmer? First, they can continue to sell through the open market but the market can be made to work more efficiently. For example, markets can be improved to provide for selling according to strict specifications – livestock markets now emphasize carcass grading to ensure prices reflect more accurately the market demands. Possibly the standards could be set by a public authority and be legally enforceable. It would also be possible to phase market supplies in a more orderly manner to meet changing seasonal demands, so avoiding large price fluctuations.

Second, farmers can combine horizontally to form buying groups or producer co-operatives.[1] The aim of these institutions is to obtain higher incomes for their members via the advantages which occur with large-scale organizations. On the input side they attain lower unit costs through economies of scale in the purchase of feed grain, fertilizer and other inputs, and larger credit facilities than farmers are likely to obtain individually; their large size also enables them to offer technical assistance on improving production techniques. With respect to marketing the co-operative has, broadly, two methods of raising the revenue of producers. First, they can continue to enter contractual arrangements with food processors and manufacturers, but through their large size and improved bargaining power negotiate higher prices than can individual farmers. They may also be able to impose greater discipline on producers, who in their initial experience with contractual arrangements may be tempted to sell through the open market, rather than fulfil the contract, when the open market price is above the contract price, which will cause diseconomies for food manufacturers and processors where stability of an adequate throughput is essential. Second, co-operatives may expand vertically into subsequent stages of production. Whilst this has happened in the case of a number of commodities, such vertical integration is far from widespread.

There are a number of reasons why horizontal farm-level integration has not been followed to any large extent by vertical integration: a high degree of coordination with both

1. The U.K. government in 1967 established The Central Council for Agricultural and Horticultural Co-operation with the purpose of stimulating the development of farmers' co-operatives and operating a grant scheme to aid co-operative activities.

production and marketing decisions resting primarily with the managers of the co-operative is probably necessary if the enterprise is to be viable economically (the Sunkist oranges co-operative in California being an example). Farmers may therefore be left with no more control, although probably higher returns, than if the vertical integration were to be undertaken by the food manufacturer, and therefore they may not wish their co-operative to expand vertically. Vertical expansion will also lengthen the time period between incurring production costs and receiving revenue, in that the co-operative will only obtain revenue on the final sale of the product, whereas the farmer, if he chooses to sell on the open market, can obtain payment soon after harvest. This may adversely affect farmers who need revenue quickly to meet regular mortgage repayments even though by waiting longer they would receive higher incomes. However, as the co-operative gains financial strength this problem can be overcome, the co-operative making its members an interim payment immediately on receipt of the product and then a further payment on final sale. A further reason for the lack of vertical expansion may be simply that the capital requirements and requisite technological know-how present high entry barriers to the co-operative attempting to establish processing factories.

Before leaving vertical integration we should dismiss a misunderstanding which sometimes arises concerning the market power and stability which results from this institutional arrangement. It must be noted that market power does not derive from vertical integration *per se*. Rather, market power, for example the ability to exploit input suppliers or consumers of the product, grows out of the degree of integration, or concentration at the given *horizontal* stage of production (see Mueller and Collins, 1957). Thus, merely because a farmers' co-operative growing, say, oranges, is vertically integrated into processing, distribution both to the home and export markets and advertising this does not give it market power. Rather the co-operative will only achieve market power in an area if it controls the production of a significant proportion of the oranges consumed in that area. By restricting supply the co-operative may then be able to obtain higher incomes for its members. If it does not control a significant proportion of supply, as would be the case for citrus fruits in the United Kingdom market where no one country supplies all U.K. needs, competing imports entering from the U.S.A., Spain, Israel and other areas, then the market power of the co-operative is essentially limited to the degree to which its product is differentiated in the eyes of the consumer.

Marketing Boards

So far, two methods by which farmers may increase their income, vertical integration and producers' co-operatives, have been examined. A third method is the marketing board as set up by legislation in the United Kingdom. In the United States marketing orders may be established. In this section we indicate aims of marketing boards and trace their welfare effects, that is, we attempt to determine whether farm incomes are raised at the expense of the middlemen in the marketing chain or rather at the expense of consumers. In view of the fact that producer marketing boards can lead to significant income redistribution these monopoly institutions need careful study. Generally, society is wary of granting monopoly power, as that power may be abused; therefore we also examine whether the methods by which producer marketing boards pursue their ends could be achieved voluntarily, rather than necessitating the creation of a monopoly organization.

A marketing board may be defined as 'a producer-controlled, compulsory, horizontal organization sanctioned by governmental authority to perform specific marketing operations in the interests of the producers of the commodity concerned'. The over-riding objective of any board is to improve the long run incomes of its members, although this objective may be masked by the use of such phrases as 'orderly marketing' or 'fair and reasonable prices'.

Marketing legislation dates primarily from the interwar period; it was deemed necessary for two interconnected reasons first, the impact of the world slump in the late 1920s and 1930s, and second, the failure of the more orthodox voluntary marketing co-operatives to halt the decline in prices and incomes, let alone restore them to previous levels. In this section we are primarily concerned to indicate the methods by which marketing boards can raise incomes, but reference is made to specific country legislation or board operation where it illustrates the underlying theory.

Broadly, marketing boards may raise producers' incomes in three main ways. First, they may help *reduce on-farm production costs* by encouraging greater farm efficiency and through bargaining with input suppliers. Whilst boards do engage in these activities they are not normally considered to be the main functions of a board and will not be considered further here.

Second, producer-boards attempt to *shift consumer demand* for their members' product through, for example, quality control, advertising and provision of new outlets. These methods have been successful in a number of instances: for example, the Israel orange export marketing board expanded the demand for their product through quality control and differentiating the Jaffa brand by advertising. In general, however, the aggregate demand for food products is inelastic because of the physical constraint imposed by the fact that we can only eat so many meals per day, and advertising campaigns may therefore lead to competitive advertising at retail level between home supplies and imports and/or between different commodity groups; in which case, rather than expanding total consumer demand, the advertising may well be self-cancelling. However, granted some advertising is necessary, for example defensively on the part of a home producer, does this compel the formation of a monopoly producer board? Broadly, all that is necessary is a method of collecting advertising dues to cover the promotion costs, and this hardly requires the establishment of a monopoly organization.

Third, and most important, producer marketing boards can raise farm incomes by maximizing returns from a given demand There are a number of methods by which this objective may be implemented, among them the following:

Countervailing power. One method of raising farm incomes is to reduce the supernormal profits of factor suppliers or firms in the final product market. The disparity in the market power of agriculture and the oligopolist buyers of agricultural output was a major reason for the U.K. Agricultural Marketing Acts of the 1930s, which established a number of producer marketing boards. However, the mere fact of high concentration in say milk distribution and milling coupled with low farm prices for milk and wheat is hardly enough to demonstrate that farmers are subject to exploitation by the firms in these industries; evidence of predatory conduct on the part of these processors and distributors, to the detriment of agriculture, has generally not been forthcoming. In fact the structural characteristics of the food-manufacturing industries are such that they are unlikely to be able to operate for any length of time an oligopoly agreement which enhances their own incomes and lowers those of the product producers. Especially important here is that entry barriers into food manufacturing are low: optimum plant size is not large in relation to market size; and the absolute cost advantage of existing firms is not large in that specialized know-how, patents, product differentiation and control of necessary inputs do not make for significant entry barriers. Thus whilst the firms in the product market might be able to gain supernormal profits at the expense of agriculture in the short run, such profits would probably be eroded quickly by new entrants.

Where oligopoly power does exist, the agricultural sector could, through vertical integration, itself enter the market. This combination by farm-firms to counter oligopoly power is generally considered reasonable and could possibly be achieved by voluntary combination at the farm level followed by vertical entry into food processing and distribution in competition with other firms at that horizontal stage. Again, the dominance of buyers might be based on producers' lack of knowledge regarding market opportunities; in this case the cure is provision of more market information and the establishment of a better grading system. These two measures were both important in the U.S. in reducing the superior market power of the large meat packers; similarly in the U.K. the Fatstock Marketing Corporation has undertaken extensive market research to determine what the consumer really wants and is instrumental in transmitting this information back to producers. However, if entry barriers into the food-manufacturing sector are high and exploitation of product producers widespread it may only be possible to counteract this oligopoly or monopoly by a statutorily established compulsory organization of producers, whose collective bargaining position will be significantly enhanced by having control of total output although even this may not lead to a reduction in middlemen's margins. Rather, the two parties might come together to maximize joint profits at the expense of the consumer, as occurred under an agreement between the Milk Marketing Boards and milk distributors in the U.K. prior to the Second World War.

An additional method of raising farm prices by reducing oligopoly profits amongst food manufacturers occurs if a board is able to introduce greater competition in the selling mechanism of the product; thus the board itself does not engage in bargaining; rather it ensures that there is more competition amongst buyers at each sale. Canadian marketing boards have successfully introduced greater competition in the selling mechanism for tobacco and hogs. Another example, although not one which occurred at the instigation of a marketing board, has been the squeeze on food manufacturers' and processors' profit, possibly to the farmers' benefit, caused by the backward entry of supermarket chains into direct competition with those firms at that horizontal level.

Competition with existing firms. Marketing margins may be eroded if marketing boards perform certain marketing functions, for example assembly and storage, in competition with firms in the product market, providing the board is successful in lowering unit costs. In fact, marketing boards have generally not attempted to compete with these private firms in providing marketing services, partially because they depend on the cooperation of the processors and distributors and do not wish to incur an adverse trade reaction. Generally, increased marketing efficiency has stemmed from competition among private firms rather than between firms and producer co-operatives. However, if producer-incomes can be raised by competing with processors and distributors it is unnecessary to delegate compulsory regulatory powers to a marketing board. Rather this producer gain can be exploited by voluntary producer co-operatives. This has the further advantage that if in fact the producer co-operative finds it is more efficient for private firms to undertake the marketing functions then it will let these firms do so, whereas a marketing board may still undertake the functions, and subsidize the relative inefficiency from the income it receives from the sale of the product.

Direction of the product. Marketing boards may be able to enhance producer prices by directing the output through the marketing channels such that total handling costs are minimized. However, as has been pointed out, 'Boards have made little attempt to influence marketing channels or methods . . . and have evinced only perfunctory interest in securing the movement of products into consumption by the shortest route and in bringing about an optimum organization of marketing facilities with respect to scale, technology, location and operation' (Warley, 1963).[1]

Generally, marketing boards have been unsuccessful, or not interested, in eliminating excess capacity, duplication of services and cross hauling. In some instances the operation of marketing boards has led positively to inefficient resource allocation; for example, if a board pools transport costs the locational advantages held by producers in different geographical areas are rendered perverse, those with the most favourable locations directly subsidizing the incomes of those unfavourably located.

Supply control and discriminatory pricing. The remaining methods by which marketing boards may raise producers' incomes require compulsory control of producers' output.

1. This article provides an extended discussion of most of the points made here.

These instruments are, first, supply control, which can take two forms. Most severely, in the face of inelastic demand, the board can deliberately restrict supply over a long period, thereby enhancing incomes. Less severely, prevailing prices may be maintained in the short run by declining to market a short run surplus, caused perhaps by favourable weather conditions. Second, discriminatory pricing, that is, equating marginal revenues gained from sales in different sub markets which are separable by time, place or different uses to different consumers and have differing demand elasticities; for example, households pay a higher price for milk than do food manufacturers, reflecting the more inelastic demand of the households. This enables the total revenue to be gained from the sale of the product to be maximized. This price discrimination frequently masquerades in marketing legislation under the phrase 'orderly marketing'.

It is necessary for the boards to exercise compulsory control over the output if they are to restrict supply or practice discriminatory pricing because the industry approaches the perfectly competitive model. Thus farmers who refused to participate in supply restriction or controlled distribution would act in their own (short-run) self-interest and assume a completely elastic demand for their output at the high price gained by the marketing board. On the basis of such an assumption they would expand output, and industry output would be increased beyond that which maximized the joint revenue of all producers (i.e. industry revenue) leading to price reduction and an equalization of prices in the separate markets.[1]

1. The seriousness of failing to control total supply depends of course on the number of producers outside the control of the boards. One farmer in such an atomistic industry, expanding output by say ten times, would have only an infinitesimal effect on total industry revenue. However, if a larger number of producers remained outside the board's control in anticipation of each facing an infinitely elastic demand schedule at a higher price than previously, then the supply control scheme is obviously doomed to failure. This is the 'fallacy of composition', i.e. what is reasonable and sensible for one producer in isolation from the others is not sensible if similar actions are adopted by all or even a significant proportion of the other producers. The reason that the

The major impact of enhancing farm incomes through these methods is likely to fall on the consumer. Certain individual middlemen may receive lower income due to a reduction in handlings, but income transfer will primarily be from consumers to farmers, in the form of higher consumer prices. It is because of the possibility of higher consumer prices through supply restriction or discriminatory pricing that the actions of producer marketing boards need careful scrutiny. Generally, the other instruments by which marketing boards attempt to raise producer incomes are considered reasonable[1] but society is somewhat more concerned about monopoly power being used for supply restriction to the detriment of consumer welfare. However, the evidence on this suggests that consumer welfare has suffered only in a relatively small number of cases. In North America supply control is 'seldom used either by marketing boards in Canada or under marketing orders in the United States' (Wood, 1967). In the U.K. hop producers have adopted limited quotas, but the welfare effects of this are of course negligible, hops constituting some 2 per cent of the final price of beer. More importantly, milk consumers have had to pay a

---

Marketing Board requires compulsory powers to exercise supply control is similar to the reasoning behind the fact that lighthouses, defence, etc., are provided publicly, through the exchequer. Assume an attempt was made to provide defence expenditure through voluntary contribution: virtually all individuals would say to themselves 'I shall receive the benefits whether I contribute or not, therefore I shall not pay my share.' It is therefore left to the government to provide these services, from compulsorily raised exchequer revenue.

1. The reasonableness or otherwise of the policy measures taken by the marketing boards remains, of course, a value judgement, but few would condemn the following: attempts to improve the efficiency of the distribution system; attempts via countervailing power to erode supernormal profits obtained by oligopolistic food processors and manufacturers; attempts to shift the demand function for their product to the right; attempts to mitigate the short run surplus–deficit production problems caused by over-response of quantity produced to price changes, which produce the cobweb cycle so familiar in agriculture. This statement would probably still hold if compulsion was necessary to finance their actions. (For details of the cobweb cycle in agriculture see Shepherd (1962), pp. 124–6 and Allen (1959), ch. 4.)

relatively high price mainly because of the operation of a discriminatory pricing policy by the Milk Boards. As a broad generalization however, it may be stated that agricultural producers have not used supply control to exploit a monopoly position, whether they operate through marketing boards as in Canada and the U.K. or marketing orders as in the U.S. There are two main reasons for this.

First, and most important, to maximize revenue through restriction of supply it is necessary to control total supply. The producers patently do not have such control in the countries we are considering. Thus in the U.K. imports of most food products are freely allowed and this would offset attempts at supply restriction.[1] In Canada marketing legislation is a provincial responsibility and in the U.S. marketing orders tend to be granted to producers in different areas. Under these circumstances the producer generally does not have control of total supply, with the effect, for example, that a marketing order which set a relatively high price for milk in the Michigan milkshed induced entry of milk from Detroit and other surrounding milksheds.

Second, marketing legislation typically places constraints on the operation of the producers. In the U.K. the Milk Boards, which have a monopoly in liquid milk supply, no imports being permitted, are subject to control over distributors' margins and consumer prices by the Ministry of Agriculture. The U.S. legislation permits representatives of middlemen on the Administrative Committees which operate the orders; and the U.K. legislation permits Ministerial intervention and requires that appointees of the Minister of Agriculture sit on the Boards together with the elected producers' representatives, these ministerial appointees being chosen for financial and commercial capabilities and knowledge of consumer affairs. Similarly, food manufacturers and distributors have a right to be consulted on the operation of the board; also the legislation

1. This statement must be qualified to the extent to which home producers are successful in getting the authorities to delay granting import licences, as they have been in the case of potatoes.

requires consumer committees to represent consumer interests and report on the workings of the Act.[1]

Let us now draw together the threads of the argument. Marketing boards or marketing orders aim to raise producers' incomes; they can pursue this end in a variety of ways, some of which do not require compulsion, e.g. more efficiency in the marketing chain, whilst other methods do, e.g. supply restriction. Any transfer of income to farmers will come primarily from consumers rather than handlers, except in the cases of exercising countervailing power to erode the monopoly profits of the oligopolistic food manufacturers or taking over certain marketing functions. Society is primarily concerned with cases of supply control and discriminatory pricing which do require compulsory membership by producers and where there is a danger of substantial redistribution of income away from consumers in favour of farmers; however, generally producers have been unable or reluctant to exploit their monopoly position in such cases. Nevertheless, despite the fact that consumers have not in general been subject to adverse income redistribution, it is worth re-emphasizing two points which have run consistently through this section. First, efforts to raise incomes through voluntary co-operatives are entirely legitimate and encourage greater efficiency in the marketing of agricultural products, that is, if the present system is inefficient. Second, we must remain wary of granting compulsory powers to producers under marketing boards or marketing orders. Compulsory legislation may be required under certain circumstances, but now that farm incomes are supported publicly via institutions such as the Commodity Credit Corporation in the U.S. and methods such as deficiency payments in the U.K. (see chapter 7) there is less need for measures which can maximize agricultural producers' revenue via supply restriction; thus legislation should only require all producers in an area to be parties to an agreement if there are adequate consumer safeguards such as the possibility of imports or direct ministerial intervention.

1. See *A Comparative Study of Agricultural Marketing Legislation in Canada, Australia, United Kingdom and the United States*, A.E./64–65/11, University of Guelph, Nov. 1964.

7 Agricultural Policy

Virtually all advanced countries operate some form of support policy for their agricultural sectors. A fair array of reasons exists for this support, and methods of implementing agricultural support policies are numerous. In this chapter, we describe the objectives of support policies, and then provide a framework to categorize the different methods of implementation. This framework is filled out by drawing examples from the agricultural policies of the U.K., U.S. and Western Europe. The chapter concludes with a brief appraisal of policies, emphasizing that it is only recently that the problems of the agricultural sector have been understood to be fundamental, requiring structural adjustment, rather than merely transitory problems requiring temporary income support.

Objectives of Agricultural Support Policies

To raise farm incomes

Increasing farm incomes is probably the major single reason for support policies in advanced countries. Measures to reduce the disparity between farm and urban incomes which would require substantial exchequer support are not normally undertaken in under-developed countries mainly, because agriculture is so large a sector in the economy and income support would involve extensive use of government revenue which policy makers judge would be more beneficial in alternative uses. However, under-developed countries can and do support their agricultural sectors by methods requiring little or no government revenue, such as supply restriction and buffer stock policies.

The agricultural sectors in advanced countries are characterized by four features which, taken together, make for relatively low agricultural incomes. These four structural features are:

(1) the demand for agricultural products is often inelastic with respect to both prices and income,

(2) a rapid rate of technical change,

(3) the structure of the industry approaches the classical concept of perfect competition,

(4) historically, the resources in the industry especially labour have not been sufficiently mobile, and have remained in the sector despite lower returns than they could obtain in alternative uses.

Viewing first the supply side, we find that a rapid rate of technical progress coupled with a near perfectly competitive industrial structure results in a continuous rightward shift in the industry supply schedule. The rapid technical progress in the agricultural sector derives from the research effort of both public and private institutions, for example, input suppliers. However, the mere existence of this rapid rate of technical change does not guarantee a shift in the supply schedule: the technical improvements also have to be adopted by farmers. They are taken because of the competitive structure of the industry.

The early innovators find it profitable to use these new or improved inputs for they are able to sell their expanded output at existing market prices, thereby increasing their incomes. As more farmers adopt the improvement, industry supply increases. This rightward shift in the industry supply schedule, when coupled with a demand schedule for the industry output, which is inelastic with respect to both price and income, results in a reduction in the market price of the output.[1] This reduction in price will be reflected in a reduction in income for those firms

---

1. For the diagrammatic exposition see Lipsey (1966), ch. 22. It should be remembered that the demand for agricultural products is not always inelastic. For example the demand for domestic production of import substitutes and the demand for many agricultural exports is relatively elastic.

whose output has not expanded. This in turn leads to pressure on the laggard firms to adopt the innovation in an effort to expand output and/or lower their unit costs, shifting the industry supply curve further rightwards and again lowering market price. It is now that the competitive system runs into difficulties.

This reduction in incomes should lead to an exodus of resources from the industry; but this exit from agriculture has never manifested itself at a speed sufficient to attain equilibrium between incomes in the agricultural and industrial sectors. The productive resources in agriculture are relatively immobile. The fixity of land and farm buildings is understandable as, except for agricultural land on the fringes of urban areas, these factors are so specialized that their return in alternative uses is relatively low; also they are fixed physically and therefore cannot be moved to a more convenient location. The labour input is somewhat more mobile than land and buildings but migration from agriculture, whilst large absolutely, has not proceeded sufficiently quickly or far enough to equalize farm and non-farm incomes.

The economic variables influencing migration were discussed in chapter 2[1] and here only those factors making for fixity are mentioned. First, rural areas may be located a considerable distance from the areas of alternative employment; this means that the flow of information to the farm labour force about job prospects and relative wages may be imperfect; also potential earnings must be discounted for the cost of moving out of agriculture. Second, the skills which farm people possess may be of little value in other industries. This is likely to be especially true for older farm workers who, should they succeed in finding alternative employment, might receive a return below that which they presently attain in agriculture. Third, there exists an inverse relationship between off-farm migration and the business cycle, with labour backing up on the farm when industrial unemployment rises; moreover, the potential earnings must also be discounted if 'last hired – first fired' agreements

1. For a more extended discussion of the factors making for fixity of resources see Hathaway (1964).

are in operation in the industries to which migrants move. Finally, it may be that both farmers and hired agricultural workers are prepared to accept lower incomes because of what they consider to be the non-pecuniary advantages of remaining in the agricultural industry, such as job satisfaction and love of the countryside.

The problem of rigidity is perhaps more pronounced in the United States than in the United Kingdom as the U.K. has a larger percentage of hired farm workers, who are more mobile than family farm people. Nevertheless, the fundamental problem is the same for both countries; namely, to achieve a greater measure of equality between the incomes of people employed in the agricultural sector and those in the industrial sector it is necessary to significantly hasten the out-migration of labour from agriculture. It is because this adjustment has not proceeded with sufficient speed that methods of increasing agricultural incomes have been devised.

To reduce wide fluctuations in agricultural prices

The fundamental causes of violent fluctuations in agricultural product prices are similar to the causes of relatively low incomes. The volume of production is likely to vary unpredictably from year to year according to weather conditions. The relatively long gestation period in production (especially livestock) makes it impossible for the industry to react quickly to changes in consumer demand. Whilst fluctuations in price are perhaps not so serious as persistently low incomes, it is likely that some firms will lack resources to withstand more than a short period of low prices without reducing production expenditures. This is especially so if farmers have to sell their output immediately after harvest (and therefore probably at a relatively low price) to, for example, repay mortgages or pay input suppliers.

To protect consumers

In times of war the authorities frequently control or fix the price of basic foodstuffs to protect urban consumers against very high prices caused by scarcity. This protection of urban interests and concomitant reduction in inflationary pressure is often a major objective in present less-developed countries where urban workers, whilst a minority in the country as a whole, form a vociferous group, likely to cause political discontent if food prices are not controlled.

As an incentive to increase production

There are a number of reasons why price and support measures are used to stimulate production. First, under-developed countries may want to stimulate production to raise nutritional levels and to keep pace with the likely rapid growth in consumer demand; they are of course constrained in how far they can support farm prices by the fact that the government expenditure does have alternative uses, especially aiding capital accumulation in the industrial sector. Whilst more advanced countries are not experiencing such rapid population growth as the less developed areas, they nevertheless have a second reason for using price and support measures, namely, to achieve a selective expansion in particular commodities in line with expected changes in consumer demand.[1] In these cases there is therefore an emphasis on changes in kind rather than quantity. To achieve selective expansion the price of the commodity whose production is to be expanded is raised relative to other farm prices, or alternatively certain inputs used in the production of the commodity (for example nitrogenous fertilizers in the case of livestock) might be subsidized.

The third reason for utilizing farm income support measures to expand production occurred in Western Europe immediately following the Second World War. The expansion of European agricultural production was encouraged because of the precarious balance of payments situation which most Western European economies experienced in the immediate post-war period, particularly the shortage of dollars. They therefore

1. See particularly the U.K. *National Plan*, Cmnd 2764, H.M.S.O., 1965, for details of the selective expansion programme of British agriculture.

used support measures to expand home agriculture and save on imports.[1]

Fourth, production may be expanded to increase exports of agricultural products. Whilst it is true that price and support measures will stimulate production and exports this does not necessarily mean that the revenue of an individual exporting country will rise for they are frequently unable to exert any major influence on price levels prevailing in international markets. That is, they are price takers, and their export revenue depends not just on the quantity sold but also on the world price, which may be falling if world supply is increasing rapidly. A measure of control over world price can be achieved via international commodity agreements but these might be difficult to negotiate if there are a large number of producers. The only countries who are able to influence world price and hence export revenue, are those who control the major share of the world supply in a particular commodity, for example, Brazil regulated the world supply of coffee via a buffer stock policy in the years prior to 1940.

To improve efficiency

To keep pace with the technological improvements of the industry, farmers must use increasingly bought-in inputs and mechanical methods. They are only likely to undertake this capital deepening if they have an assurance of reasonably stable prices for some time in the future. Also without these guaranteed prices the farmer may not be able to make his demand effective because of lack of funds. Increasingly, however, methods which do not involve higher farm prices, such as amalgamation of small farms, are being used to encourage efficiency.

It is now necessary to turn to the actual methods of implementing agricultural price and income support policies.

1. The idea that agriculture contributes to import saving and so makes a net contribution to the balance of payments is still implicit in British agricultural policy; this notion has been the subject of much controversy. The European Economic Community has also continued to encourage an expanded agricultural sector with a view to becoming self-sufficient in foodstuffs.

Methods of Supporting Agricultural Prices and Incomes[1]

Measures to support agricultural prices which do not involve price guarantees

Although price guarantees were widely adopted in the 1930s, measures to raise prices had been prevalent for a considerable time prior to the depression. Even when guarantees were widely adopted, these older methods of supporting agricultural prices were normally retained or alternatively were modified to implement price guarantees.

The regulation of international trade. Import duties and tariffs are used widely to protect home industries and need not be analysed here. From the viewpoint of raising agricultural prices, import duties are normally termed levies. Import quotas on agricultural products became important in the 1930s, providing very effective protection for domestic agriculture. Variants of the import quota method occur in specific cases; for example, the U.K. at one time limited the entry of fruit when home production was at a peak. Also the U.K. now uses a quota system on, for example, butter, to achieve an equitable balance between home, traditional and new foreign suppliers and to stop dumping. Some countries also operate a system of minimum import prices (m.i.p.s) on certain commodities; that is, they are not prepared to give access to imports if the price falls below a certain level. The U.K. operates such a system in the case of cereals. Whilst m.i.p.s have the advantage (in addition to giving protection to home agriculture) of being easy to administer, they may have the disadvantage that the importing country has to pay out more foreign exchange than if it was prepared to buy at the lower world price. Specifically, the country will have to pay out more foreign exchange if the elasticity of demand for imports is less than one. Therefore, the

1. It is impossible in the limited space available to take account of all the variants of measures to support agricultural prices and incomes. Here therefore we concentrate on the basic mechanics of policy, with reference especially to Western Europe and North America. For a more detailed analysis of the policies see Food and Agricultural Organization, *An Inquiry into the Problems of Agricultural Price Stabilization and Support Policies*, Rome, 1960.

higher are imports as a proportion of the total production of a given commodity, the more inelastic the demand for the imports is likely to be, and the greater is the probability of an increase in foreign exchange out-payments compared with the level of foreign currency payments when the importing country bought the commodity at the world price.[1]

An additional method of raising domestic prices is through a two-tier price system: to support the domestic price any excess supply, after home demand has been satisfied, is disposed of abroad, possibly in the form of aid, at a lower price.[2]

The organization of marketing. Farmers' co-operative marketing organizations and statutory marketing boards are also used to support prices. These organizations strengthen the position of farmers in bargaining with input suppliers, food manufacturers and the government. If the organizations pool receipts this adds to the security of the individual farmer who might otherwise receive a lower price because he sells at the wrong time or in the processing rather than human consumption market. These organizations increasingly use modern management techniques such as market research, enforcement of quality standards, and advertising campaigns both to stimulate consumer demand and to aid in forecasting the future quantity and quality requirements of consumers. The growth of co-operatives has been most striking in Scandinavia; in Denmark their efficiency has enabled its agricultural sector to compete effectively on world markets with those of other countries which receive a significant measure of public support. In Sweden, for example, farmers' co-operatives handle 99 per

1. In the U.K. case the m.i.p. for cereals has been the subject of much controversy as the U.K., at a time when the balance of payments was in serious adverse disequilibrium, negotiated a system which could have raised the price it paid for cereal imports to a level well above the world price. For a discussion of this problem see Peters (1965).

2. It is also possible to use a two-tier system in the domestic market. In the U.S. the government shifts demand by subsidizing school lunches. In the U.K. the school milk programme was developed partly because of an excess supply of milk. Both of these policies have beneficial secondary effects in terms of improving nutritional levels.

cent of milk output, 74 per cent of meat and eggs and 60 per cent of bread grains.

Statutory marketing boards are used widely in the Netherlands and U.K., but mainly as a tool for implementing price guarantees. However, it should be noted that these bodies may raise prices through intervention in international trade. The best example is afforded by the Canadian Wheat Board which is the sole marketing agency for all wheat, oats and barley grown in Western Canada. Producers receive an initial payment (fixed in the light of market prospects) when they deliver grain to the elevators. Later in the year they receive an interim and possibly final payment on the basis of the pooled returns obtained from sales in both Canada and abroad.

Agricultural price guarantees: types and examples

The idea of guaranteeing farmers a price was introduced temporarily in the U.K. in 1917 for cereals and again in the depression of the 1930s. The earliest comprehensive legislation was introduced in the 1930s in the U.S. based on the concept of *parity*, that is, with the aim of maintaining the real purchasing power of agricultural products equal to that of the base period 1910–14. Price guarantees became widespread during the Second World War both to stimulate production and to support farm incomes.

Measures to provide farmers with a price guarantee are operated by both governments and private industry. Statutory guarantees are of two major forms, guaranteed minimum prices and a guaranteed price range.

First, *guaranteed minimum prices*: this is the most widely used form of price guarantee, typically administered by intervention to control market supply, reflecting the fact that more advanced countries are generally prepared to tolerate high consumer food prices in an effort to eliminate part of the disparity between agricultural and industrial incomes. The system is primarily concerned with producer interests as it does not interfere with the market mechanism to protect consumers when high prices prevail, but instead lets these high prices generate a response in supply. Conversely, it does protect farmers from the effects of a sharp fall in the market price, via government purchases, usually through a body like the Commodity Credit Corporation (C.C.C.) in the U.S. or a restriction on imports.

The C.C.C. affords a fine example of the mechanics and problems of attempting to support prices by intervention to restrict market supply. It was established early in the New Deal and authorized to support the price of selected farm products at some pre-announced level; broadly, the support price is 90 per cent of parity price.[1] The C.C.C. administers the system by acquiring that proportion of output that is necessary to maintain the market price around the support price. It was realized that the system would only work successfully if combined with some form of output control and in the 1930s first acreage allotments and then marketing quotas were introduced. Nevertheless, by 1939 substantial stocks had been accumulated, but because of the war-time expansion of demand the C.C.C. was able to sell these stocks at a profit. Similarly the C.C.C. accumulated stocks in the immediate post-war years and again sold a portion of these profitably in 1950 owing to the increase in demand generated by the Korean war.

After 1952 farm output expanded rapidly and the C.C.C. had to enter the market increasingly to maintain the support price; this resulted in further efforts to control supply and reduce surpluses. Marketing quotas and restrictions on planted acreages were reintroduced, and in 1954 Public Law 480 was passed which enabled foreign countries to purchase stocks in their own currencies, rather than in dollars, and provided for grain shipments to ease famine and other disasters abroad.

Despite these measures, stocks continued to rise and in 1956 the Soil Bank was introduced. Under this programme farmers were paid for reducing their acreages of the major supported crops below the acreage allotments, or reducing total cropland acreage provided they left the land released from production

---

1. The rigidity of this method of determining support levels was one of the causes of surplus problems in grain. In the U.S. the parity price calculations up to 1956 overvalued crops (for which demand was declining) and undervalued livestock products (for which demand was increasing).

idle. Whilst around 30 million acres were taken out of production in the peak year (1960) the over-all aim of the policy was unsuccessful because it appeared to overlook the fact that land is only one input in agriculture; farmers, as rational beings, merely retired marginal land and cultivated the remaining acres more intensively. At the peak carry-over year, 1961, 1·4 billion bushels of wheat were in storage (over twice annual domestic consumption) and 2 billion bushels of maize (about six months' output). In the early 1960s the total cost of support was running around $4 billion per annum and the problem of running down stocks and raising farm incomes appeared as distant as ever (Hathaway, 1963).

The case study of the U.S. problem provides empirical support for two *a priori* hypotheses about the operation of buffer stock policies which are used primarily with the long-run aim of supporting incomes rather than as essentially a short-run mechanism which adjusts seasonal variations in supply. First, buffer stock policies are likely to lead automatically to surplus problems. Farmers know they can sell all their output at a price maintained above the true market price and are likely therefore to continue to expand production; the U.S., for example, was only able to reduce stocks owing to exogenous factors such as war-time shifts in demand and Indian famine relief, the secular trend of inventories being upward. This leads to the second generalization: given that buffer stock policies tend to lead to surpluses, substantial funds must be set aside for storage, insurance, depreciation and interest in addition to the sums available for purchasing the commodities at a level above the market price. In the U.S. in the early 1960s the interest and storage charges alone were $1 billion annually (equal to half the $2 billion loss on disposal). This also implies that buffer stock policies may be totally unsuitable instruments for supporting incomes in tropical countries whose products are perishable, and where storage and refrigeration is far more difficult than in the temperate zone.

Guaranteed prices can also be achieved through *financial* methods, rather than by exercising control over supply. The U.K. system of deficiency payments succeeds in lessening the distortion of the market mechanism as compared with other support methods and combines low food prices to consumers with guaranteed prices to farmers. This is only possible, however, because the U.K. is a substantial net importer of food – consumers pay the (low) world price and farm incomes are raised by a handout which equals the deficiency between the guaranteed price and the average returns received from selling at the prevailing market price. Thus the burden of supporting farm incomes is shifted entirely from the consumer to the exchequer; as the U.K. operates a progressive taxation system this has the favourable effect of ensuring that farm incomes are not bolstered from the pockets of low-income families (who pay no, or little, taxation) and who otherwise would perhaps have to cut down food consumption, lowering nutritional levels.

A further advantage of operating a deficiency payments system is that the amount of the transfer payment is not masked in any way but rather appears as a specific item of government expenditure. This facilitates a more objective appraisal of the level and distribution of support than is possible using other support methods. Consider Figure 10.

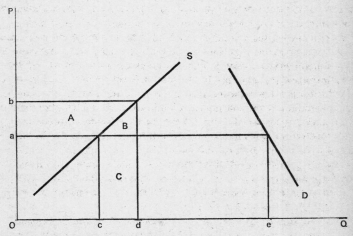

Figure 10   Market for a good subject to a deficiency payment

At world price Oa home supply equals Oc and home demand equals Oe. In order to both reduce imports (= ce) and transfer income to farmers a subsidy per unit of ab is put on home supplies, which induces an output increase of cd. Therefore foreign exchange equal to area C has been saved, and the cost to the exchequer of the deficiency payments is A + B.

In the U.K. the drain on the exchequer resulting from 'open-ended' deficiency payments, that is, on the total home output of a given commodity, induced successive governments to, on the one hand, limit the number of units of a commodity on which the deficiency payment was to be made, and, on the other hand, limit the amount of the subsidy per unit. The former is achieved by limiting the deficiency payment to a 'standard quantity' of the commodity in question, where this is determined by acreage or yield. Standard quantities presently operate for barley, bacon and milk. The extent of the subsidy per unit of output subsidized is limited by reducing the difference between the guaranteed price and import price, either by reducing the guarantee or raising the import price, by negotiating m.i.p.s with our suppliers.

The second legislative method of price support is via a *guaranteed price range*. Methods of guarantee which involve a range provide protection for consumers against very high prices in addition to insuring agriculture against very low prices. The best example of a guaranteed price range is the system of price setting for cereals, milk and butter in the European Economic Community, which provided the prototype for the Community's agricultural market organization. It is possible for individual product prices to fluctuate between a *target price*, set in theory to give a fair return to the more efficient producers, and a *support price*, from 5 to 10 per cent lower than the target price, below which prices are not allowed to fall. A *variable import levy* ensures that imports of farm produce are not offered on the internal market at less than the target price. Prices are supported internally in precisely the same way (and with similar problems) as the C.C.C. operates in the U.S. If the price on the internal market falls below the target price the European Agricultural Guarantee and Guidance Fund can buy on the open market to support the price. If the price falls to the support level, it *must* buy everything offered to it at that price. If the price rises above the target price the Fund will sell stocks and imports will enter.[1]

Some producers of certain commodities have in recent years also been provided with the prospect of a guaranteed price through vertical arrangements with manufacturers. This vertical integration may take the form of actual ownership of the farm by the food manufacturers, which reduces the farmer to the status of a hired operative. The more widespread form of vertical linkage is of a contractual nature, the farmer maintaining the major proportion of the entrepreneurial functions of managing the farm but contracting to supply around a specific date a certain quantity/quality of the commodity in question. This type of contractual arrangement has developed furthest in the U.S., especially for broilers and hogs but is also becoming increasingly important in Europe. The form of price guarantee varies between firms and commodities but will be in the nature of a minimum price or a price range. Despite the growth of privately negotiated guarantees the major method of implementing guarantees remains via the government or a government agency, and therefore contractual arrangements will not be considered further here.

Non-price methods

It is often stated that the alternative to supporting agricultural incomes by raising prices is to reduce costs and improve production efficiency. However, this is only part of the picture; measures which raise aggregate productivity may *ceteris paribus* reduce agricultural incomes per head because the percentage reduction in price, due to the rightward shift in the supply schedule superimposed on an inelastic demand for agricultural products, may be greater than the percentage change in output.

1. For a fuller description of the E.E.C.'s agricultural support methods see the *Economist*, March 13 1965 and *Common Agricultural Policy of the European Economic Community*, Cmnd 3274, H.M.S.O., 1967.

Therefore measures to increase productivity, if they are to raise incomes, must be accompanied by policies which encourage necessary agricultural adjustment, especially encouraging mobility of farm labour, or some form of guaranteed price. Having appended this rider we can now turn to the more important cost-reducing, productivity-increasing policy instruments.

One method, common to many countries, is to *subsidize the purchase of inputs* making the net price to the farmer less than the true market price.[1] Such schemes not only reduce costs but may also be used to encourage the innovation and adoption of new or improved inputs. Where economies of scale are only attained at high levels of output the initial subsidy, if successful in fostering a more widespread use of the innovation, will result in lower unit production costs and in time eliminate the need for the subsidy. This was the rationale behind the original Indian fertilizer subsidies; and similar reasoning was invoked in the U.S. where farmers were not asked to pay the true capital costs incurred in the provision of electricity to rural areas.

It must be noted that where governments do subsidize inputs they must ensure that they are not held to ransom by manufacturers who collude to raise prices in the knowledge that any price increase they make will not affect demand as it will be offset by a higher rate of government subsidy payment maintaining a constant net price to the farmer.

Many countries are now attempting to raise agricultural productivity and incomes by changing the most fundamental feature of their agriculture, namely the *agrarian structure* itself. This structural reform may involve the breakup of large estates or plantations but in the advanced western world the emphasis is more at the other end of the spectrum, that is, on measures to consolidate fragmented holdings and enlarge farm size. It is generally believed that structural reform to produce a unit of

1. In contrast, some agricultural support policies raise the price of the agricultural inputs. For example, maintaining the price of feedingstuffs above the true market price causes increased costs to livestock farmers.

'viable' size is necessary if agricultural incomes are to be raised.[1] In discussing briefly the experience of individual countries it will be evident that merely improving the agrarian structure by itself will do little to facilitate growth in incomes; complementary measures such as improved credit facilities and security of tenure for remaining farmers must accompany the structural changes if farmers are to have the necessary incentive and ability to utilize the best technological practices. The structural improvement typically implies a reduction in the farm labour force so policy measures which ease the shift from agriculture to industry are also needed. Thus Germany and the Netherlands, for example, which are both undertaking programmes of enlargement and consolidation have diversified their rural economies, in an effort to provide non-farm work in the mainly rural areas.

In Sweden farm rationalization is viewed as a long-run policy which will improve the income level of the industry in the future rather than immediately. The policy is implemented by only guaranteeing income parity with urban income levels to farms of a certain *norm* size. In 1959 this norm size was increased from farms which could support one full-time worker to those which could support two (equivalent to twenty-five to fifty hectares of arable land or 100 hectares in the southern plains region), which was considered to be the minimum size for farms utilizing modern technology. In this way a very definite spur is provided to encourage external rationalization; once the farm is potentially economically viable capital is provided on favourable terms for improving land and buildings and purchase of more technically efficient inputs. The comprehensive Swedish labour retraining system also abets rationalization as displaced workers will be less deterred from leaving agriculture if facilities

1. Whilst in chapter 4 it was stated that evidence on economies of scale is sketchy the fundamental point for advanced countries, from the viewpoint of raising incomes rather than production, is not one of economies of scale *per se* but rather increasing the land–man ratio to ensure that the farm unit is of a size viable enough to be able to adopt the most up-to-date technology and farm practices, or at least ensuring that the land owned (or worked) by one individual is one consolidated entity and not fragmented over a wide area.

exist for them to be retrained with the skill-mix required by the present expanding industries.

Legislation was also introduced recently in Britain to provide funds to aid the amalgamation of farms. A grant equal to half the cost of combining is made where the amalgamation scheme produces a 'commercial' farm (defined as 600 man-days per annum) under single ownership. This amalgamation is being encouraged by giving grants or annuities to outgoing farmers, which should go some way towards solving the problems posed by older workers who remain in the industry because it is difficult for them to get alternative employment which would yield as much as their, albeit very low, return from agriculture.

Agricultural incomes may also be supported directly by measures such as remission of taxation or direct subsidies, for example those payments made to hill farmers in Britain and marginal milk producers in Sweden. More indirectly, land improvements and technological measures such as research, education and extension, and provision of technical services such as artificial insemination should help to produce more efficient farm units and so enhance the prospect of increased agricultural incomes.

Appraisal of Agricultural Support and Price Policies

In addition to appraising support measures from the standpoint of the farmer, it is necessary to gauge the beneficial or detrimental effects which they have on consumers, international trade and general societal welfare.

Insofar as the major objective of support measures in contemporary advanced countries is to reduce fluctuations in, and raise the level of, *farm incomes* we may take this objective as our starting point. The support measures will, of course, only raise aggregate farm income and iron out fluctuations in this income to the extent of the support umbrella; the more widespread the coverage, the greater the protection. Whilst it is true by definition that price guarantees protect farmers against wide fluctuations in prices, these support policies alone will not stabilize income. Farm incomes have two components, price and quantity sold, and support measures only pertain to the former. It is for this reason that supports and measures to reduce production costs, if their aim is to achieve parity between agricultural and industrial incomes, frequently go to those who need them least. The small farmer (in terms of gross output rather than land stock, which may be extensive but of poor quality) having a lower output will gain proportionately less than the high-output farmer, who is likely anyway to be relatively more efficient and therefore less in need of the subsidy. However, society may gain from the fact that the bulk of the transfer payment goes to the large farmer who will have a lower marginal propensity to consume but rather will plough funds back, raising productivity and food output.

Price supports may affect *consumption* of foodstuffs if they are implemented by restricting market supply (as in E.E.C. and U.S.) so raising price, rather than financially (as in U.K.). This will mainly affect low income groups who spend a significant portion of their incomes on food. The influence of farm price supports on consumption will also vary between commodities. If the agricultural product is processed extensively, for example wheat for bread, the farmer's share in the retail price is so small that variations in the price the farmer receives will have little effect on retail prices. Rather it is for unprocessed livestock products such as meat, poultry and eggs where the farm price is a higher proportion of retail price that variations in guaranteed price will substantially influence consumption. This is accentuated by the fact that these products also have the highest price elasticity of demand amongst the range of food output.

Price supports which lift domestic price above world price are likely to both cause an increase in domestic supply and reduce domestic demand, so increasing the probability of surplus production. This implies that countries operating these supports will export more or import less than if the world price prevailed; given that high price supports for income purposes operate in advanced countries this may lead to *restrictions on international trade*, or more specifically, limit the prospects for poor countries to finance their development effort by increasing agricultural exports; this is especially serious in view of the fact that underdeveloped countries tend to have a comparative advantage in the production of natural resource based goods; also the immediate prospect of an increased flow of aid seems limited.

Whilst this brief appraisal has only picked on certain aspects of agricultural support it does provide the key to the whole underlying problem facing agriculture and emphasizes the fallacious reasoning evolved by policy makers in attempting to cure this problem. The fallacies stem partly from the fact that agricultural policies have frequently been formed in an emotive environment which regards agriculture as a way of life, rather than more objectively, viewing it as merely one industry in a country's economy. Also it was because they failed to understand that the underlying disparity in incomes between agriculture and industry cannot be cured by piecemeal tampering with the market mechanism, but are more fundamental, requiring an adjustment in the resource structure of agriculture. Specifically, when agricultural incomes are raised by increasing agricultural product prices or reducing costs this merely accentuates the underlying income problem, making it more profitable for existing resources to remain in the industry, thereby accentuating the rigidity of the sector.

Instead the problem should be viewed as one of adjustment. The rapid rate of technical progress coupled with an inelastic demand for food will continue to exert downward pressure on agricultural prices. Broadly therefore there exist two ways to reduce the disparity between agricultural income and industrial income. First, to deliberately slow down the extent of research and rate of agricultural technical change. However, this option is unlikely to be tolerated by society. We must therefore turn to the second alternative, improvements in the agrarian structure coupled with policies to significantly speed up the rate of outmigration from agriculture, if the agricultural adjustment problem is to be solved.

References

ALLEN, G. C. (1959), *Agricultural Marketing Policies*, Basil Blackwell.

BAIN, J. (1951), 'Relation of profit rate to industry concentration', *Quarterly Journal of Economics*, vol. 65, no. 3, pp. 293–324.

BAUMOL, W. J. (1962), *Economic Theory and Operations Analysis*, 1st edn, Prentice Hall.

BISHOP, C. E. (1961), *Economic Aspects of Changes in Farm Labour Force*, Iowa State U.P.

BROWN, L. R. (1965), 'Increasing world food output', *Foreign Agricultural Economics*, no. 25, U.S.D.A.

CAVES, R. (1968), 'Market organization, performance and public policy', *Britain's Economic Prospects* (ed. Caves), Allen and Unwin, ch. 7.

CAVIN, J. P. *et al.* (1963), 'Agriculture and economic growth', *Agricultural Economics Report*, no. 28, U.S.D.A

CHAMBERLAIN, E. (1933), *The Theory of Monopolistic Competition*, Harvard U.P.

CHRISTENSEN, R. P. (1966), 'Population growth and agricultural development', *Agricultural Economics Research*, vol. 18, no. 4.

CLARKE, J. M. (1940), 'Towards a concept of workable competition', *American Economic Review*, vol. 30, no. 2, pp. 241–56.

CLODIUS, R., and MUELLER, W. (1961), 'A report on market structure research in agricultural economics', *Journal of Farm Economics*, vol. 43, no. 3, pp. 515–53.

COWLING, K., and METCALF, D. (1965), 'An analysis of the determinants of wage inflation in agriculture', *Manchester School of Economic and Social Studies*, vol. 33, no. 2, pp. 179–204.

COWLING, K., and METCALF, D. (1968), 'Labour transfer from agriculture: a regional analysis', *Manchester School of Economic and Social Studies*, vol. 36, no. 1, pp. 27–48.

COWLING, K., and PERKINS, R. (1963), 'Producer behaviour in the choice of sugar beet varieties: comparison of game theoretic solutions with actual selections', *Bulletin of Oxford Institute of Statistics*, vol. 25, pp. 109–17.

CROMARTY, W. (1959), 'The farm demand for tractors, machinery and trucks', *Journal of Farm Economics*, vol. 41, no. 3.

GEHRELS, F., and WIGGINS, S. (1957), 'Interest rates and manufacturers' fixed investment', *American Economic Review*, vol. 47, no. 1, pp. 79–92.

GRILICHES, Z. (1957), 'Hybrid corn: an exploration in the economics of technical change', *Econometrica*, vol. 25, no. 4, pp. 501–22.

GRILICHES, Z. (1960), 'Measuring inputs in agriculture: a critical survey', *Journal of Farm Economics*, vol. 42, no. 5, pp. 1411–21.

GRILICHES, Z. (1963), 'The sources of measured productivity growth: U.S. agriculture 1940–60', *Journal of Political Economy*, vol. 21, no. 4, pp. 331–46.

HART, P., and PRAIS, S. J. (1956), 'Analysis of business concentration: a statistical approach', *Journal of the Royal Statistical Society*, vol. 119, no. 2, pp. 150–90.

HATHAWAY, D. (1963), *Government and Agriculture*, Macmillan.

HATHAWAY, D. (1964), *Problems of Progress in the Agricultural Economy*, Scott Foresman and Co.

HATHAWAY, D., and PERKINS, B. (1968), 'Farm labour mobility, migration and income distribution', *American Journal of Agricultural Economics*, vol. 50, no. 2, pp. 342–52.

HEADY, E., and TWEETEN, L. (1963), *Resource Demand and the Structure of the Agricultural Industry*, Iowa State U.P.

JOHNSTON, B. F., and MELLOR, J. W. (1961), 'The role of agriculture in economic development', *American Economic Review*, vol. 51, no. 4.

JOHNSTON, B. F. (1966), 'Agriculture and economic development: the relevance of Japanese experience', *Food Research Institute Studies*, vol. 6, no. 3.

JONES, G. (1963), 'The diffusion of agricultural innovations', *Journal of Agricultural Economics*, vol. 15.

KUZNETS, S. (1961), 'Economic growth and the contribution of agriculture: notes on measurement', *International Journal of Agrarian Affairs*, vol. 3, no. 2, pp. 1–25.

LATIMER, R., and PAARLBERG, D. (1965), 'Geographic distribution of research costs and benefits', *Journal of Farm Economics*, vol. 47, no. 2, pp. 234–41.

LEWIS, W. A. (1954), 'Economic development with unlimited supplies of labour', *Manchester School of Economic and Social Studies*, vol. 22, no. 2, pp. 139–91.

LIPSEY, R. G. (1966), *Introduction to Positive Economics*, 2nd edn, Weidenfeld and Nicolson.

MATTHEWS, R. (1964), 'Some aspects of post-war growth in the British economy in relation to historical experience', *Transactions of Manchester Statistical Society*, 132nd session, pp. 1–25.

METCALF, D. (1968), 'Concentration in the retail grocery industry', *Farm Economist*, vol. 11, no. 7, pp. 294–303.

METCALF, D., and COWLING, K. (1967), 'Demand functions for fertilizers in the United Kingdom, 1948–65', *Journal of Agricultural Economics*, vol. 18, no. 3, pp. 375–86.

METCALF, D., and GREENHALGH, C. (1968), 'Price behaviour in a retail grocery sub market', *British Journal of Marketing* (Autumn), vol. 1, no. 3, pp. 243–51.

MEYER, J., and KUH, E. (1957), *The Investment Decision*, Harvard U.P.

MINISTRY OF AGRICULTURE (1968), *A Century of Agricultural Statistics, Great Britain, 1866–1966*, H.M.S.O.

MOORE, J. R., and WALSH, R. G. (eds.) (1966), *Market Structure of the Agricultural Industries*, Iowa State U.P.

MUELLER, W., and COLLINS, L. (1957), 'Grower-processor integration in fruit and vegetable marketing', *Journal of Farm Economics*, vol. 39, no. 5.

MUELLER, W., and GAROAIN, L. (1961), *Changes in the Market Structure of Grocery Retailing*, Wisconsin U.P.

PETERS, G. (1965), 'A note on minimum import prices', *Farm Economist*, vol. 10, no. 11, pp. 466–9.

ROBINSON, J. (1933), *The Economics of Imperfect Competition*, Macmillan.

ROGERS, E. M. (1958), 'Categorizing the adoption of agricultural practices', *Rural Sociology*, vol. 23, no. 4, pp. 345–54.

ROGERS, E. M. (1962), *Diffusion of Innovations*, Free Press of Glencoe.

SCHULTZ, T. W. (1953), *The Economic Organization of Agriculture*, McGraw-Hill.

SCHULTZ, T. W. (1964), *Transforming Traditional Agriculture*, Yale U.P.

SCHUMPETER, J. A. (1942), *Capitalism, Socialism and Democracy*, Allen and Unwin.

SHEPHERD, G. S. (1962), *Marketing Farm Products*, 4th edn, Iowa State U.P.

SOSNICK, S. (1958), 'A critique of concepts of workable competition', *Quarterly Journal of Economics*, vol. 72, no. 3, pp. 380–423.

TRIFON, R. (1959), 'Guides for speculation about the vertical integration of agriculture with allied industries', *Journal of Farm Economics*, vol. 41, no. 4, pp. 734–46.

VINCENT, W. H. (ed.). (1962), *Economics and Management in Agriculture*, Prentice-Hall.

WARLEY, T. K. (1963), 'The future role of marketing organizations', *Journal of Agricultural Economics*, vol. 14, no. 4, pp. 550–71.

WAUGH, F. V. (1964), 'Demand and price analysis: some examples from agriculture', *U.S. Dept. of Agriculture Technical Bulletin*, no. 1316.

WITT, L. W. (1965), 'The role of agriculture in economic development – a review', *Journal of Farm Economics*, vol. 47, no. 1, pp. 120–31.

WOOD, A. W. (1967), 'The marketing board approach to collective bargaining', *Journal of Farm Economics*, vol. 49, no. 5, pp. 1367–75.

Index